MW01277876

OUT
AND
BACK

ESSAYS ON A FAMILY IN MOTION

For Mark -
who'll have lots
of stories!

Published by Atmosphere Press

Cover design by Beste Miray Doğan

atmospherepress.com

OUT AND BACK

ESSAYS ON A FAMILY IN MOTION

ELIZABETH TEMPLEM

Elizabeth Templeman

atmosphere press

♥

For Matilda

and Ada

and Isabel

and Grace

... and the ones who follow.

♥

Contents

TAKING FLIGHT

It sounds like distress. We're canoeing along the far side of Heffley Lake, my husband and I, when we hear the cries, sharp and raucous. Straight above us, we see an osprey lunge and rise. She spirals around the bank rising from the lake edge, her calls growing more insistent. We can't help but sense the alarm, and then wonder if *we* might be the cause. My husband spots the nest, high above in a pine that leans out over the water. Then, one scrawny neck, thrusting the head up over the edge. Moments later, impelled by the unmistakably shrill irritation of a parent, the young bird tumbles out and drops into flight. It takes us a moment to comprehend what we've witnessed: first flight.

We paddle beneath, leaning to watch as the pair of them swoop and glide, adult circling widely and then shepherding the young one back to the nest. Once more she coaxes her chick, this time with less fuss. Again they circle, but further from the bank. I can hardly breathe for the wonder of what we're watching. Imagine, taking flight for the first time; and imagine, coaxing your offspring to do so. How do you gauge the day? The moment? The capacity for a safe return? But then, perhaps these are not wholly unlike the tests we face, in our awkward, earthbound ways.

**

It was a hot evening in August, fifteen years ago, when we drove to Horseshoe Bay to meet the ferry bringing our daughter back from a week with a long-boat flotilla along the Sunshine Coast. She was fifteen. It was a late sailing, and a hot night.

I felt a stir of joy to see her step off with the other passengers; and then a rush of anxiety as I took in the patch covering her right eye—a startling contrast to the glow of her tan and the grime coating both girl and backpack. She stunk of sweat and salt, dirt and dampness. But more surprising than those accumulated effects of a week camping with a group of teens—or the patched eye— was some elusive and more fundamental change in her: She exuded confidence. It was so distinct, and so astonishing. I took in the muscled arms and shoulders and a new huskiness in her voice. I couldn't get enough of her and as we drove home, twisted to see her there in the back seat, at first full of stories and then overtaken by drowsiness.

In fact, the injury and the change of voice were short-lived; but the sense of strength—a kind of easing into herself—never really left. Maybe it was always inside her, and the adventure—being away from home, challenging herself physically, acquiring new wisdom—brought it to the surface. Whatever prompted the transformation, it was the start of her finding her wings and moving away from us. I think she had to come back, to recognize the shift. (Or that's me, wanting *our* role—and the return to us—to matter.) She would take other trips and has always been drawn to adventures. And she'd seem a bit different upon each return home, but never so dramatically, in my eyes, as when she stepped back on the mainland that hot August evening.

Her brother's solo flights were many, and though we thought we'd been through this, the quality of the anxiety and the ache of separation were different with him. He first left us, after high school graduation, to work at the oil patch, to earn his way to Europe. He departed in the midst of a turbulent time for him, and for us. He'd been pushing against us for years, testing our limits, tolerance, love. His leaving seemed more deliberate, and as much about getting away as about seeking adventure. He left within two days of his eighteenth birthday, a sunlit morning in July, pulling out in his ancient and battered vehicle with what seemed a potent mixture of relief and regret. I thought my heart would break as he disappeared down the laneway.

Five months later, on Christmas Eve when he drove back up our driveway, he was transformed. A restless, lanky child had left; a hardened young man returned—ruddy with windburn, and with a pierced tongue. As he leaned back into the embrace of a living room chair, the stories rose one from the next. His laughter came easily and he radiated confidence. That buoyancy characterizes him to this day.

Since then, he's made his European trek, and lived to tell the tales. He survived the years away at university, with all the stories we know, and those we don't. But like his sister, he was transformed by that first flight.

I remember being keenly aware of how their younger brother was hanging back, just waiting to try his wings. It was hard to miss the agitation, the tremors of turbulence growing. His time was coming. I knew the event would be marked by discovery—for him and for us—and by apprehension, too.

The fear is real; the danger, too, is real. Taking flight is as laden with peril for our kids as for the young osprey. And once they stretch those wings, the nest becomes more launch pad than home.

GETTING THERE

We tend to consider travel in terms of destination. That's the focus when we plan, budget, and dream. But travel is both: the being there *and* the getting there. For a family of five, travel is often much more about the getting there.

My husband and I began taking annual road trips when our kids ranged in age from one to eight. Starting with Vancouver, then Seattle, and Victoria—as the children grew, our destinations extended to Barkerville, and another time, Drumheller. In ever-increasing trajectories from home, we made our way to Long Beach, and down to the Writing on Stone Provincial Park on the Milk River in Alberta.

These were wonderful trips, each one set off by memories of the journeys back and forth—of carsickness, backseat squabbles, a lost wallet, a flat tire, plans gone awry and routes gone weird. Each destination becomes a gem in the family tapestry, with its own cut and hue; but the journeys to and fro are no less distinct and remarkable.

***

In the summer of 2002, we took our most ambitious trip. Our family was hovering on the brink of inevitable change:

our oldest, entering Grade Twelve, the youngest nearly ten and the middle one in the thick of teen-hood.

For two years we planned this trip, only half in jest when we coined it "Trip of a Lifetime." Because we are a family not accustomed to a leisurely life—travel "for travel's sake" seeming a bit presumptuous to us—we attached solemn purposes to our trip: to look at colleges, to visit our aging parents, to instil in our kids a sense of their country.

Leaving home on July 14th, we set out north and east toward Edmonton, and made our way—through six weeks, nine provinces, seventeen thousand kilometres, sixty-five hundred dollars—to the farthest tip of Cape Breton Island, around, and back to the southern interior of BC.

We anticipated sharing adventures and discoveries. Which we did. The surprise was how—amongst our collective memories and stories—the road-stories would predominate. They could have happened anywhere, maybe even to any family; but they happened to *us*, becoming part of the history that defines us.

***

Our means of travel was a rented, gleaming white Ford Windstar. Despite my husband's resistance, bags and packsacks, pillows and books all came onboard. We transformed 136 cubic feet into a nest with caves into which the kids would burrow. Only the driver could fully extend both legs.

As individuals, we are active, with strong, disparate personalities, so it's not surprising that together we are less than harmonious; our seatbelts enforced a pattern of proximity, allowing only a finite set of variations.

Sometimes we'd travel in silence, responding to some unspoken but shared sense that quiet was what we needed. Those spells would get broken by one of us, triggered by whatever transpired outside the van: boot inverted on a fence-pole; sign proclaiming, "Home of Chicken Chariot Racing"; a speckled hawk. Then we'd drift into a buzz of conversation, laughter, or quarrel.

Most often we'd travel to the background of music or radio. Our increasingly divergent tastes left only four CD's we would all tolerate. For hours each day, we'd roll along—visibly unified, eyes trained forward on the undulating hills of Saskatchewan, or the rocky wilds of Northern Ontario. But closer inspection would reveal that the three kids were enveloped in their own aural universes, each with their discman bought especially for the trip. Yet, in my favourite hours, The Barenaked Ladies, the Beatles, Miles Davis, or Neko Case blasted from the van's speakers.

We devised complicated ways to pass time, which turned into simple pleasures we shared. There were the things we counted: stretch limos, hometowns of hockey players, pink houses. And things we competed to notice first: chip trucks, a change of weather, church steeples. And the debates to determine finest beach, best breakfast, cleanest restroom.

***

At home we tended to occupy prescribed roles, to assume identities defined by our habits and clutter and familiarity. We lived in the grip of schedule and routine, balancing our colliding interests and needs. Despite cohabiting a space, there were days we'd barely see one another.

If Annie Dillard is right when she claims that schedule "defends from chaos and whim," then surely travel casts the family straight *into* chaos and whim. Travel means flux and unfamiliarity. Away from home, we're challenged to define ourselves differently, reacting and adapting as we jostle against one another in new and complicated ways.

I remember thinking about how to maintain some semblance of schedule for our travel so the kids could grasp the shape of each day, even when much of what filled the day would be unknowable and new. Some would be designated as driving days, punctuated by meal stops and a night out of the vehicle; or rest days, where we'd be in some place which would become, temporarily (and often at quite an effort), home. Giving them choices for how we filled the time helped, too. They'd take turns deciding things like where and when we'd eat, which made for some interesting experiences (and spread the responsibility for the inevitably bad decisions).

***

En route in our Windstar, we discovered who we were, in this interlude of unaccustomed constraint, and freedom. I discovered that it's usual for one of us to sink, as another rises. Tempers flare, and then settle. The ire of space invaded—foot resting on a violin case, elbow pushing against shoulder—disrupts a precarious serenity. Panic erupts; accusations fly—a lost retainer, a missing bag of spits, spilt juice—and as suddenly fade. One will fidget; another will make allowances.

And then, harmony: Nicole, the oldest, teaching her brothers, to their delight, a game called Asshole. They played for hours, killed themselves laughing. This was the first of our card-playing, which outlasted the trip, becoming a tradition.

***

On the road for days, we found an astonishing variety of ways to irritate one another, but also to buoy the collective spirit. We'd form strange alliances and make elaborate compromises: once trading an hour to meander along a stretch of coastline—an hour's drive for nothing more than a glimpse of Cape George—for a movie in Halifax; and another time a hike for a Subway lunch in Digby.

We made it through the tough patches, in the process living the stories that would outlast all the adventures and souvenirs we'd gone seeking. Consider these two—one from getting there, one from returning.

***

It's late afternoon of day three, and we're determined to make good time. The deadline is a cottage rented in New Brunswick for the week which begins on Andrew's 14th birthday. A more immediate target is brunch at the best pancake house in Canada, which we'll find in Thunder Bay, according to what we'd heard on the radio. So we drive, from Yorkton, Saskatchewan, through Manitoba, and across the provincial border—where everyone piles out for the obligatory photo—into Ontario.

But this day has been long, already twelve hours. We're sweaty and hungry and crabby. The boys are provoking their sister, and us. In Ignace, we're finally defeated by hunger, the late hour, and the kids' restlessness. While we argue about what to find first—room or meal—it grows darker and more desolate. Shelter wins. A drive around the roadways that traverse the Trans-Canada in Ignace reveals not a single vacancy. Hunger takes over and we find the one restaurant still serving what turns out to be surprisingly decent food.

Midway through our meal, uneasy at the notion of driving onward into the darkness of this sweltering night, I return to the parking lot to phone the number of an English River motel praised in a tattered magazine clipping I carry. The man who answers sounds weary, but promises to hold his last room.

***

The 58 kilometre stretch of highway from Ignace to English River traverses what is surely the most godforsaken landscape in Canada. From the blackness, bugs slam into our windshield. Near midnight, we pull off the highway and into our motel. A man sits on a door ledge, cigarette dangling from his lip, bug spray in hand.

This *has* to be the motel of my article: It's all there is to English River. But surely the management has changed—or deserted. Been slaughtered maybe.

My husband, rejuvenating the moment the van has shuddered to a stop, hops out to settle the details. There's not a breath of air moving, and so he leaves his window down. Out of that stillness, in the instant it takes me to turn the key in the ignition to close his window, our van has been invaded by mosquitoes. They form a thrumming cloud we have to squint against, covering our noses so as not to breathe them in.

It takes all the discipline of a military manoeuvre to find night-time packs and a sleeping bag for our luckless daughter who gets the floor tonight. Despite impressive coordination and hustle, there's an unmistakable drone in the room. The boys, by now invigorated to the point of giddiness, swat mosquitoes while we take turns showering.

Though I am certain sleep will not come in this dingy room, in this eerie place, it does. I awaken to see Mont standing at the foot of the bed, towel wrapped around his waist, finger to his lips, camera in hand. I'm numb with tiredness, so silence is easy.

***

In the photo he snapped, you can make out the boys, conjoined and tangled in a sheet. James's head enveloped by Andrew's armpit, they appear as a single creature: one head, arms and legs skewed every which way. The other thing you'll notice is how the sagging mattress is patched with duct tape. We never noticed, then.

But by the light of day, blood-spattered walls aside, the place doesn't look half bad. Astonishingly restored as we drive out of English River, we're eager for Finnish pancakes. It's six A.M. of Day Four, and we're only 185 kilometres from Thunder Bay.

The second story bears a direct relationship, and proximity, to the first. We're on the way home, and determined to maintain the spirit of the trip. The van, impossibly more stuffed than when we'd left, has begun to stink slightly. Our collection of heart rocks rattles, and the kids can barely see one another, engulfed as are they by the stuff we carry.

This has been designated another Major Mileage Day. We're up early; checked out of our motel barely ten hours after arriving there. The route we're following was mapped out by an uncle with both a zeal for travel and a trucker's knowledge. We'll wind our way along the Michigan side of Lake Superior, turning northward onto a road called The Avenue of Pines, and then crossing back into Canada.

This will *not* be another English River day. I have planned it out with special care: reserving a room the day before, in a hotel with a pool, in Steinbach. But I've underestimated distances, and overestimated tolerances.

Just after our lunch break—a picnic on a lovely and utterly deserted beach—tension sets in. This is slow going. By dinner, assembled between a Burger King and a grocery store, moods are growing strained. Darkness has fallen, and my confidence with it. The Avenue of Pines is lovely, as promised—moonlight filtering down through spires of black trunk—though daylight may have suited it best. In any case, the boys, the younger feigning sleep, won't even look out the window.

Mont is clenching his jaw, alert every moment for deer or moose. The kids are growing silly, and loud—till I shout at them to be quiet. Then they get sullen, and I wish for silliness again. The silence, usually refreshing, weighs heavily.

Ages later we cross into Manitoba, not far from Sprague. Though I realize we're hours away from our hotel (from *any* hotel), I keep that to myself. Then, looming in the dark horizon, a sign: "Steinbach—160 kilometres." I *will* the kids not to notice. They do. James bursts into tears of such desolation that we forge ourselves into a frenzy of consolation. Snacks, music, stories, all materialize. Minutes later we are singing along to the boisterous lyrics of "One Week," by now able to keep up with The Ladies. Then we hear choking sounds from Andrew. Mont, back to clenching his jaw, bristles at this over-the-top clowning.

Nicole, ever calm, points out that Andrew *is*, in fact, choking. Turns out he inhaled a corn chip in a heroic effort to share snacks and laugh at a joke, simultaneously. The van lurches to the gravel roadside, the suddenness dislodging the corn chip. We dissolve in laughter, tears streaming down our faces. Andrew insists that this is *not* funny: It hurts, and he could have died. He's right, of course. It *could* have been disastrous, an emergency in the worst conceivable place. But in the context of the day, it's just what it will take to get us to Steinbach. We arrive just past midnight, to a clean and spacious room, and settle down for sleep; Andrew's throat sore, James's spirits fragile. For months afterwards, one of us only has to refer to Andrew as 'Chip' to reduce us to laughter.

***

Our trips constitute experiments with leisure and aimlessness, with abandoned schedules, and with forging practicality from abstraction.

From the moment we had pulled away from our driveway for that big trip, we never did miss home. Home had *become* that crowded, smelly van, bulging with our possessions. We emerged, six weeks later, cramped and yearning for privacy, yet, regretful—that particular and peculiar version of ourselves already fading. I would miss the intimacy of our five bodies, whether packed within our vehicle by day, or the nylon membrane of our tent by night. Finding food and warmth and making a home-place for eating and sleeping become so elemental. It refocuses us on what is essential for a good life. So simple, really: a good sleep, a good meal, and maybe a walk through the woods.

Months later, looking through our photos, I was struck by landscapes of dazzling blues and greens, and by what a fun family we appear against the backdrop of the Windstar. But we're so much more complicated than that. We're distinct individuals; the connections running amongst us tangled and sinuous.

Each of the kids processed the Trip of a Lifetime in their own way, in their own time. Nicole put together a scrapbook for us. James created a journal, complete with illustrations. He claimed to love "The Bug Guts Express," while not much liking the actual driving time. Andrew hung his provincial flags on his bedroom wall, along with the mask he'd bought himself at the art fair in Montreal. He also kept a ledger with a great assortment of details ("Tums and gum" under "Other," for Wed. July 17th). By week two, only fuel and major meals and motel rooms show up—along with the complete record of every hometown of a hockey star we passed through ("Churchbridge, Sask. home of Kelly Buchburger….").

***

The following summer—the oldest child by now graduated and soon to be setting out for a year abroad—we decided to complete the dream of traversing our country. We had only six days, and that the result of hard-won compromise with a son just beginning his first real job, and the daughter in the midst of relationships already pulling her from the family's centre of gravity. This would be a far shorter trip, within our province: north and west through the Chilcotin, and then down the coast from Bella Coola to northern Vancouver Island, eventually cutting inland, then east, toward home. But we never quite made it home, meeting the forest fires which kept us away for a long, tense week.

This second trip was freighted by so much less expectation: the planning less inclusive or extensive; the family less united in its conception. Yet it took on a significance we'd never have anticipated. When we were finally back home again, barely settled and still living on alert, our daughter departed for her Rotary exchange. She would return home only to leave again for the Maritimes, where she'd go to one of those universities we'd visited on Trip of a Lifetime.

***

We knew full well that she wouldn't ever be home again in quite the same sense. And that her brothers would follow her. And then, we'd redefine ourselves yet again.

Travel will likely be at the heart of that work of reshaping our identity as a family. Travel is, in a sense, the opposite of home, and as intrinsic in defining our sense of ourselves. Travel—by the very act of moving beyond home, and then back—has transformed us even as it has exposed us for who we are, each one an individual, embraced in this web of family.

BANDS

The finger third from the thumb on my left hand is ringed by a pale indentation. It itches slightly. A close look (reading glasses required), will reveal, through puckers and fine lines, a band of tiny bumps that cause, or mark, the prickliness. On the palm-side, there's one bloodspot— barely visible, but enduring.

The ring that's left this impression lies in a wicker basket, painted cornflower blue and brimming with hair elastics and whatnot, that sits on a shelf in the bathroom. Every now and then, I have to root around to be certain that it's still there. I'm prone to imagining it dropping down the drain of the sink.

The ring has, for most every day of the thirty-some years I've been married, surrounded that finger of my left hand. The thumb that gets drawn, now, to the indentation there, habitually traces the ring's surface when I'm preoccupied or restless. Two surgeries and a couple of diagnostic tests are the only things that have prompted its removal—until this year.

***

In 1979, weeks before we married, my husband and I—
then merely and hopelessly in love—drove to a jewellery
shop his mother recommended in Mildmay to choose our
rings. I had never heard of Mildmay, one of a profusion of
tiny towns dotting Southern Ontario, but I loved how the
name conjured up gentleness and spring breezes.

We chose with great care: plain bands, but distinct, to
my mind. (My search today yields an image of the exact
pair of rings on Wikipedia. So much for proud distinction.)
Monty's was gold; mine, white gold—to match a beloved,
but long-gone, bracelet of silver. Opting for that difference
felt dizzyingly radical. For us, no simple conformity,
nothing ornate or showy; for us, simple, dignified,
genuine, and, of course, affordable.

I remember those new rings gleaming brightly, sliding
onto those young fingers to reflect our new marriage.
Today, they gleam still, but not all that brightly. Mont's has
a scratch etched along one edge, no doubt from an
encounter with a power tool. The perfect roundness of
mine has given way, slightly, to oblong; this the result of
resizing to accommodate the insidious swell of arthritis.
The golden bands age with grace; our hands, not so much.

***

My husband's ring sits in the drawer of his bedside table:
unworn, but safely intact, despite proximity with hammer,
chisel, crowbar, through all manner of weather, dirt,
concrete, and caustics. I was stunned to learn that it's been
in a drawer for five years or more. Not so much stunned
that he no longer wears it, given how rough building has
been on his knuckles, his hands, his body.... What stuns

me is that I *saw* it, still can still see it, on his finger. Do I notice not what we *are*, but what I imagine us to be?

My husband: How easily that rolls off the tongue. Last October, driving along a narrow stretch of highway through the Northern Cascades, he apologized for calling me "his wife," said he shouldn't do that. That I'm not *his*. I feel cornered by the conundrum of the semantics, being wholly comfortable with my husband, and—until that moment—with calling him that. I consider myself neither possessed (in any sense); nor a possessor. And if I am either one, it's become so comfortable, so unassuming a state of possession, that I don't notice. If it leaves a mark, it's less noticeable, less chafing, than this inverted ring on my finger.

I'm puzzled, too, about what brought the whole notion of what we call one another to the forefront of his mind. Maybe it had to do with this being a road trip to celebrate our anniversary. We mark it lately with activities—biking or hiking—a concession to my insatiable appetite for motion, and his for exploration. In the earlier, kid-filled years, we celebrated with an extravagant meal and a bottle of wine a notch above the usual.

***

The indentation on my finger has likely been a long-time developing, but its irritation is new. Thank heaven for Google's fellowship of suffering, a sorority in which I am mute, but take comfort. A search reveals that I'm not crazy, and hardly alone in this. Gold jewellery, it turns out, will suddenly and inexplicably cause allergic reactions, otherwise known as contact dermatitis. The culprit is generally assumed to be minute traces of nickel, which impart strength to the gold. Some blame stress (poor stress! blamed for every affliction), with triggering the reaction; others believe the culprit to be dry or cold weather, detergents, or plain old dirt trapped underneath.

Whatever provokes finger to reject ring, the women (as most of the cyber voices on this topic seem to be) are more alarmed at the sudden onset of the reaction: Why now? What's to say that, after five, ten (or *thirty-four*) years, the body might not be reacting to marriage itself—to the source of the symbol? Funny, though, that it's more likely reacting to the element that renders the symbol strong.

I'll restore ring to finger soon. It no longer turns freely most days, but reassures me just by being there. I like the solidness of it. Its distinctiveness—the dullness, oblongness, of it—is a fitting symbol of our own way of being together. If this is bondage, it's to some human condition far bigger than we are.

CHANGING PLACES

It was an evening in June, and we were camping at the Writing-On-Stone Provincial Park, my husband and I, our three kids, their uncle, and his dog. It had been a long drive from the interior of BC to southernmost Alberta: twelve hours magnified to close to an eternity by those three kids and that dog. But by now we were spilled from vehicles and established, our two campsites punctuated by tents, truck and car, clotheslines and bicycles. For whatever convergence of landscape and circumstance, this would be one of our best family camping trips, although we wouldn't have known that then.

The chalky Milk River runs through the park, carving its way through sandstone and scrub brush. For us, it was all so exotic: hoodoos and middens, wind-rippled grasses, and skies vibrating with birdsong. Rooting around in the high grass, we startled—and were startled by—a porcupine the size of a small tank.

After breakfast the next morning, my daughter and I went exploring. I've always loved a walk, and the river beckoned. She was likely seeking a respite from the company of four males, two being loud and rambunctious younger brothers.

The morning sky was stunningly blue, the park humming with life. A faster walker, I led the way. Blessed with a sharp eye and sure compass, Nicole navigated from behind, our rudder. The path threaded over fallen logs and through grasses, alongside the imposing formations of rock and sand that typify the Badlands. It could hardly have been more perfect when—amid our synchronized footfalls, the drone of insect and bird, the steady flow of river current, our quiet chatter—a muted, staccato buzzing caught my ear. I froze. My feet stopped. My mind, however, raced, summoning rattle snake notices we'd seen posted through the park.

Never mind their advice to carry on. I was paralysed. I might have grown old there, had Nicole not calmly stepped out ahead of me and made her way past the ledge. As naturally as though it were choreographed, the daughter, fourteen, led her mother from danger. I could claim that I followed to keep her in view, drawn by the impulse to protect. But in truth, I suffered a systems crash, and she rose to the occasion. Reflecting back, I recognize it as one of those glimpses parents will have, of the person their child is becoming. What I'd glimpsed was the understated fortitude that characterizes our daughter as we know her today. There on the Milk River, though, I couldn't see much past the cowardice of her shaken mother.

***

It was a March morning when a fresh snowfall interrupted a week of mild weather. My husband was away, leaving our youngest and I sharing house and chores. James, then seventeen, was getting ready to catch the school bus. I was on my way to an early meeting. Backing out the door, I turned to wish him a good day. In reply, James told me to drive carefully. I said not to worry: I always did. "It's not *you* I worry about, Mom," he said. "It's the other drivers." Shutting the door behind me, I had topped up the dog dish and was down the driveway before fully appreciating the irony of the moment.

***

Roles change, sometimes just for an instant. Like a flash-forward, it happens when you least expect it—on a glorious walk along the Milk River or tumbling out of the house for work on a frosty March morning. But despite these previews that life affords us, I don't think we ever come close to anticipating the challenge of assuming a new role. Never mind the awkwardness of shedding that more familiar role from which we'll emerge. Despite rituals and rites of passage that surely evolved to prepare us for such transitions, I remember feeling exactly like an impostor as an incoming university student. And again as a new teacher, as a new wife, as a mother.

There might be no better example than how, in preparation for having a child, we so intentionally work at a change—one as ordinary as life itself. Yet, despite abounding intentions and ardent preparations, becoming a parent will blindside us.

Change can feel so odd, sometimes exactly like failure. The morning comes when, after years of being nurtured and guided, the child assumes the role of protector. The kids assert themselves, advancing even as we retreat, moving into competence in ways and realms we'd never have imagined. They overtake us in intellectual acuity, in taste for indie music, in social connectedness, in thirst for adventure. They take charge of car, kitchen, computer— even of one another.

Our boys teased me for my incessant nagging, my boring insistence on taking vitamins and getting enough sleep. Resisting obsolescence, maybe, I washed their socks, baked batches of cookies and worried about them, persisting beyond all reason to mother them. All the while, I inhabited the role my mother had played. My mother: who, at 90, would have *loved* to do my laundry, to cook for me. Who worried about me with barely an inkling of what my life was like. Ours was a telephone connection: My role, as daughter, was to hear about the multitude of annoyances of senior housing, about her ill-fitting dentures, and her twisting spine. "You don't know the half of it," she would say, never telling me what that mysterious other half might be. Her past was as remote, and yet surely as significant, as my present was to her.

But my role was to listen, commiserate, and share innocuous details of my children's lives, and to keep to myself my own nagging fears and preoccupations. My mother and I had changed places. And yes, the same change of role that will surely come to pass between my children and me. We've been rehearsing for years.

THIRTY YEARS AND COUNTING

We were supposed to celebrate our thirtieth anniversary with that dream trip to Italy, but I couldn't imagine leaving our youngest, or my work, just then. Our son would likely have enjoyed a few weeks without us hovering. But this would be his last year before university, and I already suspected how much I'd miss him. Why squander weeks, when we had only months left with a child still living at home?

So we compromised: two days at the Cathedral Lake Lodge, a destination we'd always postponed because of cost, or circumstance.

***

Thirty years of marriage. That summer, right out of the blue, my sister-in-law had asked how we did it: how we stayed married, stayed happy together, for so long. Kim had come through her own terrible ordeal, married for twenty-five years to a man who struggled with depression and other demons, until he ended his life in the basement of their home. He was a sweet man, funny and fun, but clearly more complicated than we knew. I owed her a truthful answer.

We were side by side in the back of a rental car, when she asked, on our way to the family reunion of my mother-in-law, who sat in front with my husband. So many ironies, I thought, contemplating our marriage from the back seat. Two of the greater challenges to our relationship would have been our mothers, and our sons. Mothers and sons: I wonder if they are the usual test of marriage.

We've built our home and raised our family in western Canada. For the first decades of our marriage, our mothers—mine from Maine; his from southern Ontario—visited annually. I was astonished to discover, in those optimistic years, how trying their visits were for me. I felt trapped, scrutinized, threatened, provoked, undermined. Not surprisingly, I was seldom at my best. When they left, I'd feel forlorn; our marriage would feel frayed.

I don't remember when things changed, or why, but a turning point was when we could admit to the challenge of each of our mothers, rather than rushing to the defence of the mothers and leaving the other—generally me—alone. My husband was a good son. He was so considerate of and attentive to his mother. To my mother, too, he was a better son than I could ever hope to be a daughter. She had a soft spot for him that I'd have envied, if it weren't such a salvation. Our telephone calls were often tense—endless accounts of the foibles and failings of all of us: me, my siblings, even my father (never mind that he's been divorced from her for 40+ years; and dead for several). But if my husband took the call, they'll joke and laugh. In the moment it took for the phone to pass from his hand to mine, the laughter and lightness would have vanished.

***

On that summer day, as I sat—knees resting against the back of the seat my mother-in-law rested against, deep in conversation with my husband—I wondered how to answer Kim's question. If I waited a moment more I probably wouldn't have to; conversation with my husband's youngest sister turns and twists rapidly, topics fleeting and only the speed constant. Like kayaking, it's fun, but not for the lazy or timid. Rising to the challenge distracted me, too, from listening to my husband and his mother reminiscing. The upcoming reunion would be, I knew, emotionally provocative for her—seeing her seven siblings and their offspring; missing her parents. She had lots to talk about—stories reaching back, expectations simmering for the day ahead.

Unsure how, finally, to answer Kim's question, I told her that maybe we were closer to okay than happy. I said it could be hard sometimes, and then remembered her ordeal. But it *is* hard. We work at it, or avoid working at it as often. On the occasions when our youngest was away—more frequent now that he was driving—we'd find ourselves without much to talk about. Once we'd exhaust the topics of each of the three kids, our work, our next planned trip, the flow of conversation would cease—still does, in fact. But the silence doesn't feel uncomfortable—not usually. I try to remember how we used to be, thirty-five years ago, in the early years of our relationship. I think we talked more; that I might have babbled incessantly—about hopes and dreams and fears which have, I hope, either matured with me, or faded. I don't remember silence, or the quality of the silence when it did surface between us.

***

That conversation with my sister-in-law was on my mind on that anniversary trip to the Cathedrals. I think we were both struggling with the reality of approaching one of those landmarks, those long-anticipated destinations: both the anniversary, and our location. I was resisting a migraine, with little success. He also had a headache, unusual for him. The combined mood was more subdued than celebratory.

The afternoon we arrived, we went for a short, easy hike. Its vistas were lovely, but not breath-taking. We were quiet, and as the hours passed I was aware of a growing sense of fatigue. By the time we returned to the lodge, my knees were weak and my legs heavy. This was *not* what I had been expecting, and the disappointment was overwhelming, exaggerated by the intimacy of our small room. Its dark wood interior gleamed, reflecting back nothing but our own moods. We wondered, aloud, if the aches and exhaustion of that hike might have been due to the altitude, but shifted our effort from the search for causes, and towards mutually denying the impending gloom.

The second morning we awoke to snow. Oddly, this cheered us both. Together, we're good at adversity, I think. We shook off sleep and dressed quickly, making our way down to the communal kitchen to pack bag lunches and fill water bottles. Enveloped by a haze of cheer, my head still ached and my stomach protested at even the idea of oatmeal. Within an hour we were ready and heading off, pretty much alone. Others sharing the lodge had slept in, waiting out the rain and snow.

As we walked into that morning's chill and dampness, I felt my headache dissipate. By the time we made our way around and above Glacier Lake, the rains had come and gone, twice, and we were in good spirits. We travelled single file. As usual, I struck out ahead; my husband followed, calling ahead to point out sights I would have missed: tamarack trees, gleaming red mushrooms, a snow-covered spire, a blue grouse, mountain goats on a distant slope. Mostly, though, we were quiet, muffled by toques and wrapped in the din of sky and forest shedding rainwater in steadily changing rhythms. Then the winds came, growing more furious until they howled, stinging our faces and whipping hair and clothes. Nothing to do but turn towards each other and laugh. We were making our way across a ridge, impossibly high above the lake we'd left two hours ago, dwarfed by the dimensions of peak and pitch. Smooth rock gave way to chunky rocks cascading down a steep slope, and once to fine white sand—silencing our footfalls, but also destabilizing them. As we descended, rock was supplanted by a carpet of pine needles.

Midway along the ridgeline, black clouds gathered overhead and the wind edged toward sinister. Squinting to keep my lenses safe from flying pine needles and sand and my own whipping hair, through the slits of my eyes I registered the muted colours of this harsh wilderness where we two silent hikers traced a ragged line, mimicking the dotted line on the map we carried.

As we made our way back, I remember thinking about our relationship. What I sensed as the hours passed, and as we moved together across the shifting landscape, was how tightly I felt connected to this other person. Throughout the trek, and especially during the tougher sections, we seldom spoke, but ours was a companionable silence. When the downhill pitch was at its steepest and the footholds most elusive, we were silent. I felt at once both on my own, and profoundly connected. I took extraordinary care with each step, in part out of a characteristic caution and some cowardice about downhill travel—but also with full awareness that a misstep would burden my partner. We were alone out here, responsible for one another's safe return. If either of us were careless or reckless or unlucky enough to twist an ankle, the other one would suffer.

I don't know if my husband was as cognisant of this as I was. I do know that it was foremost in my mind—how we took care so as not to burden one another—though I would never have spoken of it. We both know that we lean on each other, and that things have happened—and will happen—to render one of us reliant on the other. We probably had no clue about such things thirty years ago—never would have expected that crises would leave one of us in need of the other. Now, though, all these years—through surgeries and pregnancies, arthritis and accidents and a hundred vulnerabilities—we know that marriage means inevitably we will lean on one another, and that this is nearly a sacred thing, not to be taken for granted.

As for the silence that stretches between us, it begins to feel normal—and I'm not sure what to make of that. When things are good, the silence is fine. When things are bad, it can become hurtful, even hostile. Mostly, though, it's comfortable.

These are the things that I thought about, trekking along the Cathedral Rim Trail two days past our thirtieth anniversary. The more considered response to my sister-in-law's question was taking shape in my mind: We might not be anything so simple as happily married—but we are solidly married. Like this trip, our marriage has borne little resemblance to what either of us might have expected: the way is sometimes perilous; the landscapes are forever shifting; the conditions, beyond predictable. But we make way, together.

IN PLACE

It all began with Lyn. She was annoyed by our choice of theme for an upcoming conference.

This was a national conference on post-secondary teaching. Hosting it was a big deal for our small university. The theme was to be "intercultural diversity," meant to encompass diversity and acceptance in our teaching practices—surely a noble aspiration.

Lyn's point was that we're so focused on diversity, on *global* perspectives, on *internationalizing* our campuses, that we lose sight of the local: the distinct and distinguishing features of the ground beneath our feet. In a sense, we risk losing our sense of place, of where in the world we are at any given time. She showed up at my office, leaning against the door-jam, book-sack resting on her hip, exasperation lighting her eyes, maybe recognizing a shared inclination to contest the incontestable, to stir the waters now and again. We set out to draw others into what was promising to be a conversation with legs.

By the next week we were a group of four—ecologist, writer, geographer, and Canadian studies scholar—voices running over one another in a satisfying hour of discussion that flowed and diverged and converged. That national conference came and went; our group took hold and grew. We invited a historian, a visual artist, a cultural geographer; later, an anthropologist. Even as the group grew to fold in others, it would take so little to refocus, and then to forge ahead, encompassing additional perspectives. We learned that we shared no common language for place; that we perceived and designated places in remarkably different ways.

A short walk to Guerin Creek, which carves its way, unnoticed, along the southern boundary of our campus, constituted one lesson in perspective. Guided by Tom, the geographer, we searched for traces of erosion, of water accommodating the lay of the land even as the community develops over and around it. I learned to notice silt and debris, but also absences of vegetation. Together, we read the story of the landscape, noticing hue and line, linking cause and effect. Above the creek bed, along the horizon, evidence of an expanding community asserted itself.

***

Our talks represent one of the best things about being an educator: the opportunity to think and act collectively, creatively, intellectually. This group is friendly, funny, and motivated by the promise of what we might accomplish. For me, even if we never accomplish anything tangible at all, the opportunity for our exchanges and for whatever subtle shifts in thinking we might provoke will have been enough.

You might well ask why it takes six scholars to debate the essential value of place. Or, indeed, wonder how convoluted our shared academic perspective has become that we accept as worthy of contention a notion that sense of place could be anything *but* central to our human sensibility. Yet it gets argued that the upcoming generation may have evolved, intellectually and emotionally, to the extent that place may no longer be critical to identity, or family, or community, or well-being. Holding in check both despair *and* cynicism had allowed me to relish the debate, and to renew—and deepen—my own personal sense of location, and of local perspectives. As we've talked and read our way toward shared understandings, we've challenged each other to question our assumptions, those notions that, from within the safe confines of our disciplines, can take on the cloak of sacrosanct.

I learn to pay attention to how we *name* our place. Shared conventions will nudge us, without thought, to say that we work in Kamloops, this small city in the interior of BC. But how much richer with connotation, to know that I stand along the North Thompson watershed, on the sagebrush steppe within the Shuswap Highlands?

Finding our way toward a greater sense of place has been, by turns, disorienting, and exhilarating. While the differences, discipline to discipline, have surprised us, the emergence of common ground can prove as unsettling. We've come to realize that the shared pursuit of truth, a compulsion for more broadly recognized validity, may have propelled us, as academics, to privilege abstraction over the specific. From a distance, that shift seems innocuous—incontestable, even. And yet, in that quest for the sweeping certainty, have we ceased to attend to the profusion of discrete phenomena at our feet? Swept away by our own generalizations, have we lost our mooring to place?

The challenge for our little group has been finding how, within the confines of those evolving conventions and abstractions, we might restore the value of the tangible; of the abundance of minute details that distinguish and imbue with meaning the spaces we walk upon and work and play within.

***

These currents of thought have, of course, spilled beyond the confines of my professional life. I can't overlook how I've been so drawn to this group, and these explorations, because I am, indisputably, a creature of place.

At the most personal level, place is the anchor: the rich soil in which we take root; the post by which we set our compasses. All of which are metaphors for stability. And yet, among my friends and family, I am most often the one oblivious to markers of place. I know the inside of my home intimately, but only steps outside the door, the quality of knowing shifts to resemble an embracing cloud of familiar colour and texture and contours. I'm woefully ignorant about the names of grasses, flowers, and even trees—a fact made acutely evident by time spent with my ecologist friend. I mix up east and west and am capable of not recognizing our own driveway on the rare occasion when a thick fog rolls along our road. I know discrete plots of ground—the beds in my garden, my running trails, our woodpile, the dog path—but connections between them, the broader context of place others around me seem to grasp so naturally, evade me.

The siren call of my inner thoughts—the flotsam of ideas and memories, the remnants of dreams—unhitch whatever receptors might have attuned my consciousness to position. Even along my familiar running trails I will awaken from reverie with no idea where I am along the path I'm running, or which way to turn when another intersects. This has happened twice in the past year and troubled me to the core each time. And yet, despite a dysfunctional register of place, I have a solid sense of being *at home* in a place. My husband would say (*does* say) that I'm a homebody: ridiculously set in my ways, captive to routine, smitten with tradition. (And surely 'place' is the necessary ballast for ritual and routine.) He, on the other hand, has an acute sense of place and is astute in everything to do with orientation. He is also comfortable with travel, and with change; keen to explore *other* places. Years ago, we began a running argument about spending Christmas in Hawaii (his idea). On a scale of one-to-preposterous, the idea strikes me as just this side of polygamy, or voodoo. We have Christmas *here*, at home. The turkey is in the freezer, after all. And then there's our annual walk on the lake before dinner... the Boxing Day game at the rink....

***

Maybe I should try to relax, allowing myself to drift more easily, freeing myself from that anchor, or tether. Maybe this generation has it right with their far-flung companions ever at their fingertips, able to sleep wherever they put down a sleeping bag. But I know that my own kids had to grow into that ease; that it didn't come naturally to them. When they were babies, our kids would never sleep away from home. We'd notice, with some envy, how *other* parent's toddlers would slump in easy sleep—in airports, on buses, on the couch of a friend after dinner. Not ours. They'd wrestle to stay awake, sometimes nodding into sleep just as we rounded the bend toward our driveway after hours of highway travel.

I remember as though it were yesterday, an amiable late-night dinner interrupted by the clattering of the wooden beads which separated bedroom from hallway in the ramshackle trailer of our still unattached, still ski-bumming, friend. This was the sign that our daughter, barely two and assumed to be asleep in the cosy nest we'd made of her own blankets, was indeed, not so. While we finished our meal, she staggered up and down the short hallway, cradling her beloved Baby and looking for all the world like a little drunk, cheerfully unsteady on her feet.

That child would love, for an interminably long time, a book about a kitten who wandered, lost, as one after another crudely rendered farm animals would ask, "Is *this* the place where you belong?" Our daughter, assuming the shrill, high-pitched voice she bestowed on that kitten, would call out the refrain: "No, No, *No*!! This is *not* the place where I belong."

***

If I had ever doubted that place matters, and how home is its essence, raising kids would surely have restored my certainty. In elementary school, each of them had routines of homecoming. Within seconds of the back door slamming shut, backpacks would slump to the floor, and bathroom doors would bang. Home brought relief in the most visceral sense—even for the digestive track, it seems.

Emerging from the bathroom, they'd head for the fridge. Home seemed to arouse a thirst for milk. Even today, decades later, the soundtrack of their homecoming is a slamming back door, the thunderous dropping of shoes, the muted seal of fridge door, and a *thunk* of milk jug on counter.

I have my rituals of homecoming too. When I push through the door after a long day in town, an urge close to hunger is what I feel. I know it's more mental than physical—but give in to it, reaching for a cookie, cracker, or handful of dry cereal. Even before this, and less a matter of choice, twin habits of mine are to unclasp my watch and drop it in the outer pocket of my briefcase, and then to wash my hands. Only after the keeper of time is tucked away and the traces of outside are running down the drain do other cravings stir. And then I settle. A sure symptom of distress is to discover my watch missing from that pocket of my briefcase. Later, I'll find it in the oddest places—kitchen drawer, jacket pocket, front seat of car.

***

Every bit as predictable as my kids' routines—or my own— is the manner in which our homecoming is registered by our dogs. Since the kids were young, Miles, a border collie, had a unique routine to celebrate our returning home. However it may be that dogs conceive of place, they certainly demonstrate recognition of the momentous occasion of their humans returning to the home-place. While Blue, the heeler, patrolled the base of the driveway, Miles stopped at his bowl for a frantic few mouthfuls of food. Evenings, I'd extract myself and my stuff from the car to the sound of the aluminium dog dish pushed against gravel. The routine marking the return of the school bus was always more elaborate, because of its more predictable timing perhaps, or because a kid's arrival was greater cause for celebration. Who can know? As Blue would dash down the driveway to meet the bus, Miles used to tear figure eights around the property: looping around the shop, down to the sheep pens, behind the barn, up past the woodshed, and back to the house.

All of our dogs live out their lives on the southernmost several acres of our property. To whatever extent that Miles and Blue were aware of place (or of life), their awareness must have derived from the multitude of changing smells, textures, movements, and noises of our land. Included in that miasma would have been their sense of us. Just as they registered our return home, so to did they react to our wanderings. When we'd prepare for a trip, something—our preoccupation, or the packing of vehicles—would tip them off. Miles would stop eating and look what certainly could pass for depressed.

***

How could place be so ingrained in an infant's routine—indeed, seem so fundamental to even a dog's psyche—and yet cease to matter? How could we have become so sophisticated that the very notion of place becomes dispensable? It just doesn't figure. Among the articles our little group has shared is one by David Gruenewald. Drawing on other thinkers, Gruenewald argues for the distinction between the state of inhabiting a place and merely *residing* in one. Residence, he asserts, is a temporary state. When we reside in a place, we might invest little, and not surprisingly, also *care* little about that place. This brings to mind university dorm rooms (and accounts for, perhaps, the evolution of damage deposits).

To *inhabit* a place, on the other hand, implies the act of dwelling—of being at home; a far more elaborate and intimate relationship between creature and space. Fundamental to such a relationship is familiarity, and the attachment that extends from familiarity. If we appreciate the place we inhabit, we will tend to sustain it, and it, in turn, may be more capable of supporting us. That simple set of premises exposes what's at risk if we lose the capacity to know, deeply, the places we occupy in the world. It's a small step to the supposition that—if, indeed, this generation has ceased to know *how* to be attuned to place, or lacks the capacity for attentiveness required for such knowing—we need to learn to teach those things.

If the generations following us don't know how to know their place, then, despite—or because of—the years of instantaneous exposure to information and entertainment, and whatever digital communities they invoke or embrace, surely they'll suffer from a state of placelessness, or rootlessness. If this is the trade-off for becoming internationalized, for residing in a global village, I can only worry for them, and mourn their loss. I do not believe for a moment that we, as humans—never mind as a particular generation—have sufficient capacity for knowing, heart for caring, or resources for investing in place without bounds.

Human beings need home, however capable we may be of adapting to change, of picking up and creating a *new* home, or of tolerating a temporary one. If for nothing more than a point of reference for our poor extended brains—and maybe for our hearts too—we need to recognize where it is we are situated, and how to care about and to care for that place. We need names for its features, for its plants and creatures and landforms, just as we need its stories and the memories it has signified for others before us.

PRELUDE TO DAWN

The crack of dawn is magical. A dark shade of magic, balancing the light of incoming day. Dawn conjures up ghostlike hues of the palest blue, infused by grey and tinged by pink. Dawn summons the bats, their muted clamour to return to roost, even as other creatures stir from cover. Birdsong verges on frenetic. There's a buzz, a premonition in the stirring. Dawn's world hangs in suspension.

Perhaps for all these reasons, if odd things will happen in the family, the propensity is for them to happen at dawn.

Before we had kids, when I thought about it at all, I assumed babies slept through the night—and parents too. But our babies were good teachers, persistent in their unpredictability, vigorous in their ability to challenge us. Among the things I learned was that infants are most likely to grow thirsty, or bored and lonely, or feverish in the pre-dawn hours. At three A.M., an infant could be counted on to sound the nursing alarm that—even if my brain could ignore it—drew on the mammalian release of milk. In my groggy mind, it would seem as if we awoke the early bird whose solo chirping would bring in the dawn.

Now, some twenty years later, the witching hour will sometimes bring forth the dull throb behind my right eyeball, tapping out the pulse of an on-coming migraine. My migraines always lay claim to the last good hours of sleep. But that's the dark view. A brighter outlook would be that, forewarned, I have quiet hours to steel myself. Because there's a new day to reckon with, on the other side of dawn—despite headache or fatigue.

***

I have heard at dawn... neither angels singing nor dolphins laughing, but the rasping bark of croup: a sound so strange that even from deep sleep it conjured up the formidable description buried in parent handbooks.

No quiet whimper forecasting the eruption of a new tooth, this. Distinct, too, from the fitful squall that signals fever. Though I only heard the trumpet of croup once, more than twenty years ago, I don't forget the sound. Nor how I responded: as though pre-programmed, propelling myself across the floor to scoop baby from crib, charging down two flights of stairs, to the shower. I remember slamming the door, cranking on the hot water, and then the cold, to fill the narrow room with steam. I remember the chill of doubt, and then relief overtaking terror as my son, damp-faced, began to breathe like a normal baby. I remember the croaking cough that lingered, sputtering remnants of whatever croup is. The deep-chested cough of that child, now fully grown, still taps some primal fear in me.

***

I have felt, at dawn... no gentle woodland dew, but the boom of a nuclear explosion. Which daylight and reason, arriving in close proximity, will reveal to be an air horn going off in the firehouse adjacent to my father's home, calling the town's firefighters.

But alone in the guest bed, my heart beat to fill the silence between shrill blasts of alarm. And ached with longing for my kids, my husband, home.

Fear of death shrivelled in the face of that absence. Disaster, destruction, hellfire itself would have been bearable, if only I could wrap my arms around the ones I loved.

***

I have seen at dawn... the strangest of dreams, slipping from mind upon awakening; fading with the light. Our kids with ages no longer immutable.

Somersaulting through the years, freed from the grip of reality and even from shared contexts or timeframes—all three, babies one instant; the next, one's away at university, her brothers, improbably stuck in toddlerhood. One frame later, the older one drives a truck—or is it a boat? My husband and I are young and in love, our guilty lust interrupted by some inane detail—a burst pipe, a missed dentist appointment, a school play. We all slip in and out of decades. Released from the constraints of congruity and chronology, we spin backwards through the past, but never forward from this moment—bound only by whatever is the rule of dream.

COLLECTING THOUGHTS ON MEMORY

My father suffered from Alzheimer's Disease.

"Suffered" isn't quite accurate, though. Dad fell gently into the embrace of Alzheimer's. During the years between the diagnosis and his death, only once did I see him frustrated by his inability to remember. That was the evening of a visit when he couldn't remember how we wanted our steaks done. There were ten of us, so really, it was a lot to expect. But my father was a chef, and until his dying day, he was dedicated to meals—to their planning and their preparation. Sometimes, as the Alzheimer's took hold, his wife would return from work to find three different dinners in progress, her husband fretting at the freezer in their basement, searching for ingredients for yet another.

My father was not a man of intellect; nor perceptiveness—or other traits easy to admire. But he was passionate about food—seafood and steaks, cream sauces and pies. In the face of Alzheimer's, cooking gave him a sense of mastery and familiarity. For him, to forget how we wanted our steaks was frustrating, while forgetting what ages we were, or that he'd just told a story five minutes ago, seemed not at all troubling. On that occasion, our steaks were *all* cooked medium—his own preference.

Meanwhile, in my selfish heart, I fear the Alzheimer's. Will this be my father's legacy to me? I resemble him in temperament, and other ways: I have his long, crooked fingers, the thick texture of his hair. Perhaps this, too, will be mine.

The day after I learned of my father's diagnosis, I made an appointment with our family doctor to ask about what this might forecast for me. Hardly a selfless response, I know. But I was afraid.

My father was eighty-five. *He* didn't seem afraid. He seldom ever seemed to get stressed about things. He inhabited a world prescribed by simple parameters: sports, home, antiques, food. Maybe, to him, forgetting felt like less of a risk. As for me, I sensed myself skidding along a fast track of memory loss, and with so much at stake: teaching, reading, writing... Already, the gift of memory felt precious, and precarious.

***

During my father's last few years, one story he'd tell would upset me greatly. He'd tell it over and over, though I never heard the same version twice. While the context would shift to fit whichever person or year or neighbourhood came to him, the plot never changed. It went like this: There's this decent and hard-working man who enjoys his drink. He's harmless and good humoured, even when drunk. One day his wife finds his stash and smashes the bottle, spilling all the whiskey down the drain.

My father would invariably become outraged by his own story, despite the decades that had lapsed since *any* particular version would have happened. In one rendition, the couple were my maternal grandparents. It so happens that my grandfather *was* a drunk—sometimes, hushed stories suggested, a violent one. My father cast his story with many different couples: some whose names I'd remember well, or vaguely; others meant nothing to me. The story was *never* about him and my mother, but I could sense how his righteous indignation swept her into its wake.

The mere repetition offended me. That, and the unfailing sympathy for this mythical man. To me, it's the story of how my father blamed women—with their silly need for stability—for all the grief these poor sods suffered. I wanted to scream: *Don't you recognize that I am a woman? How can you assume your feelings will be my feelings? How do you reconcile the joy of a stupid drunk with the hardship of a family neglected or abused?*

I never said a word.

***

Years before, my father's careless and weak ways—products, likely, of whatever his own sketchy past had wrought—left us humiliated and penniless, again and again. This man had caused incomparable grief for my mother and had been stunningly irresponsible as a father: And then he got a second chance, with a new family. My feelings about this are muddled. I'm fond of his second wife. She became a friend and a wonderful grandmother and was devoted to my dad. I'm also fond of their two boys, although when they were kids, I resented their comfortable childhood. I don't remember my father ever noticing.

***

As for me, here is the progression of things I have failed to remember.

After our older son Andrew was born, I could no longer carry out mathematical computations in my mind. Once I prided myself on the ability to do mental calculations: kilometres to miles, litres to gallons, Canadian currency to American. Now it takes a fierce concentration—nearly brings on a headache—to hold a pair of two-digit figures in my head long enough to compute their sum.

After James, our third child, was born, a new challenge: I could no longer remember the colour of my towel. They were over-sized bath towels—my husband's pale green and mine, blue—hanging in our furnace room. One day I had no idea which was mine. At first, I simply refused to acknowledge this startling deficiency. I'd wait to catch my husband's towel damp and try to relearn. It was embarrassing, finally, to admit that I *couldn't* learn how to anchor this simple fact (green, his; blue, mine) in my brain. I could only ask, or guess. It was as though the receptacle for storing the significance of colour had been sealed. Or the code for blue and green had vanished. What was certain was how giving birth marked chunks of loss; how hormones tapped memory.

My memory for colour association did, eventually, return. (I can't, of course, remember when.) Years later, our youngest was twenty; our towels were thicker, and both the same dark green. They hung on two rods, mine toward the front—and I never seemed to confuse that fact. But I am keenly aware of how such realms of awareness can be lost, reducing a person to a dismaying state of humility.

***

For all his many faults, my father was an easy-going man—even through his dementia. A blessing for those around him. What they had to bear were the repeated stories. His mind tended toward them as water runs toward the well-worn rut in an open field.

On our visit in the year he was diagnosed, a story he kept rediscovering was about a trip to Nova Scotia from the years he'd cooked on a fishing boat. He'd tell how he'd bought kilts for my sisters, and a tam for me. I might have been three. The blue-and-black tartan of those kilts is vivid. Handed down to me, they felt special. I wore them often in grade school, clasped at the side by a pin kept in my jewellery box.

At the time of this visit, James was seven, and our daughter, the oldest, was fourteen. We were on a cross-country road trip, looping our way home from the Maritimes. At the mention of beach or boat, my father's attention would be derailed anew by the happy resurgence of his own story.

At first this scared me; it never ceased to unsettle me. I felt embarrassed for him as he relayed the same account. The kids would shift uneasily—glancing at us, or each other—unsure how to respond. Yet even the youngest soon realized that my father was wholly oblivious to our discomfort, to the repetition, to our own stories even. My father would take joy in each turn of his memory, delighted to share.

***

The awareness of forgetting is interesting—but slippery. If I pin down the intersection between remembering and forgetting, can I avert memory loss? Coming to understand—both what gets forgotten, and how it's reclaimed—may restore control. Like the sand-coloured Ginkgo pills I swallow, it might do some good—and probably does no harm.

***

The lapses of memory seem so random. I will, for example, remember that we've run out of orange juice—but *not* remember that I picked up a case. Remember the name of a movie—but not that we've already seen it and found it dreadful. Remember to make a detailed town list, but forget to take it from the counter. Or forget to put ice in the cooler so that I can get the butter home in the heat of July.

Sometimes I lose names. On trips to Vancouver, I've had trouble conjuring up the name Urban Fare, that upscale market in Yaletown. It has a wonderful array of bread, cheeses, spices. When I try to pull up the name, my mind formulates a square. (Because *square* rhymes with *Fare*?) Before I'd ever been to this market, my husband got a t-shirt as a gift. It's black, with Urban Fare written in a white block (the square?). I try to visualize the t-shirt and then read the words on its front. That seldom works. My next trick is one I've relied on for years: to work my way through the alphabet, until a word snaps into focus, pulled forth by its first letter.

Another name I'd forget caused more problems. This was Brittany, which happened to be the name of Andrew's girlfriend for a time. Her name inexplicably morphed into Tiffany. Although the kids are generally indulgent about my vagueness, Andrew took offense to this lapse. Tiffany was the name of two students I'd known. Both names have three syllables, at least as I speak them. (Kids seem to speak them in two.) Both names were common in the fifteen-to-twenty age group. My solution was to call her Britt, which came to my tongue more readily.

Why would Brittany, by any spelling, drop away, and Tiffany rise to replace it? And why would this be such a source of irritation to my son? Did he relate my forgetfulness with a lack of respect for his love life? But he was young, with lots to learn about forgetting and about vulnerability, and one's maddening lack of control over either.

Along with some place names, locations also seemed to be vanishing. I have trouble with small towns, lately, and particularly with those located on an east-west axis from home. I lose track of Clinton, Chase, Cache Creek. They slip from mind, skidding free of position. I also lose the relative positions of the seasons, sometimes to find myself frantically searching for a reminder to situate myself, (*February*: Christmas has passed; school's underway; the weather's cold) before I utter something ridiculously inappropriate to the context everyone else so blithely grasps, with not even a second thought.

***

On my last visit to see my father, he was hooked up to an oxygen tank. Tilted back in his leather recliner, he sat for hours, facing the television, wrapped in a fleece blanket decorated with footballs and team logos. The television was, as usual, on. Mostly, though, he gazed out the window, or at a well-worn photograph of he and his wife, and their boys with wives and children.

The photograph captures his second family. I am from the first. He sometimes had trouble keeping track of all of this. Most of the time he had me positioned in the first family. What he couldn't keep straight was whether I was a kid, or an adult. When I'd enter his den, he would invariably ask how "the others" were doing; when I'd last seen them. The second question led me to know that the others, in this case, were my four siblings. When he asked, his regret was palpable, and I knew he meant to convey his longing to see them.

I could never identify the trigger that would shift him to the other, more recent reality of my life, but within seconds he'd have negotiated that shift and his questioning would follow the tack of my current life: How was my husband doing? The kids? Then the protest about how long it had been since he'd seen them: When would we *all* visit? I'd answer either set of questions, despite having answered them not an hour ago. I'd feel my impatience surge, mounting to fury that this man would not face the fact of his own mortality; that there would be no time for more visits. He'd puff unevenly through the oxygen tube, fussing with the connector that fit into his nostrils, and *still* he would not recognize that I had come to say goodbye. That he would not see my husband or children again. That they were half a continent away, missing me while I was here.

My irritability would subside, trailing guilt in its path. His repeated questions left me so weary. Once I caught myself slinking past his doorway, to spare us a round.

The next morning, while making his arduous way toward the bathroom—leaning onto his walker, oxygen tank in tow—he detoured, coming up behind the computer desk where I sat reading my email. He sighed and said that he never could understand "all the fuss," with "all this computing," he supposed he'd need to learn. I wanted to roar: *You are dying! There will be no learning computers.*

But I said nothing and wondered at my smouldering anger.

***

When our family vacation folder outgrew its space on the bookshelf, I bundled all its maps and articles into a fat binder and put it in the file drawer of my desk. I made a concerted effort to memorize its location; yet the mnemonic failed. By accident, I discovered what I'd given up for lost, searching for a pencil which had dropped into the drawer: a discovery which might have been more pleasing had it been the tiniest bit intentional.

Sometimes I devise chants during my runs, threading through a sequence of chores to attend to at home (pick crab-apples, pay bills, hang laundry, water plants, make salad dressing...). But I have no method for safeguarding what sticks and what won't. The mundane tumbles with the essential, one thing summoning the next with a randomness that boggles my mind. Why can't memory sort by significance, dropping smaller items first? But no. The weekend passes: work shirt neatly mended, $4500 bill unpaid.

At other times, I will have something to contribute to a conversation: a reflection, cogent and compelling; the perfect complement to another story, and just right for this moment. But wait: The access to my story has vanished. If only I could locate the date or place or book title through which it would connect to this conversation. Instead, I lose the thread of the conversation and chase the shape of the idea which has eluded me. Even if I could track it down, I'd look the fool for slogging back up the channel to where my story could flow. Instead, I'm grounded on my private sandbar of dislocation.

***

Most sobering is realizing that I've forgotten fragments of our kids' lives. One child had nightmares about the school bus. Was that James? Two kids love canned pineapple. Which one doesn't? Nicole tells about the schoolyard collision which caused her first nosebleed, and it's a totally new fact to me.

I struggle mightily with birthdates and ages. Age changes every year, so there's logic to the challenge. (Yet I notice that other mothers seem to handle this.) Birthdays *should* be easier. May, Nicole's month, stays in mind; so why would July (Andrew's) get twisted up with August (nobody's)? And *why*, if eight arrives on cue, does twenty-one resist? For James, I remember with absolute confidence that he was *due* September 28th. That he was born on the thirtieth seems harder to retain, which is perplexing.

Once upon a time I was regarded as bright. I have considered myself intellectual and am aware that—for better or worse—I pass more time absorbed by my thoughts than immersed in the rush and tumble of life. The difference is that I used to be able to *demonstrate* that I was a person of intellect. Now, if it's even true, it's private. I know that I have an abundance of curiosity, and some imagination. But I'm not so sure that intellect thrives without memory to nourish it. My mind feels like a tangle of images, phrases, vaguely formulated ideas—most of which are impossible to articulate without more time and focus than social interaction generally permits. This makes me want to weep—or sometimes, perversely, to laugh.

***

On that final trip to see him, something extraordinary happened. Certainly, I never expected or even dared hope for such a thing. My father and I shared two moments of genuine connection.

The evening before I was to leave, he started talking about his relationship with my mother, a topic from which I'd always try to divert either of them, to stem the inevitable tide of bitterness. But this was different.

Rather than embarking on one of the usual rants, he faltered, looking baffled, and said, "I don't know what went wrong between your mother and me. Somehow we got off track." Though I can't imagine that my mother would ever have described their relationship as *on* track—

and despite his disregard for the magnitude of the eruption—I was grateful. For the briefest moment, he was admitting that he and my mother once had had something real and good between them, and that (I could be stretching here), he may have borne a share in the responsibility for its downfall. This was so far from adequately capturing the extent of his failings, and yet as close as I'd ever seen him to contemplating the reality of our family's unravelling.

The second moment that passed between us was before dawn the next morning. I was ready to leave for the airport. My father was still asleep and I was reluctant to wake him. He looked so frail on the couch, oxygen at his side: a shrunken and greyer version of the father I'd always known. And I didn't want to navigate again through the looping series of questions that would only remind me how soon he'd forget I had been there, or indeed, who I even was.

But I did wake him. It was as though he awoke before the Alzheimer's could fog his mind. His eyes shone with tears, and he told me that he knew he wouldn't see me again. He thanked me for coming and told me he felt well-loved, and then fell back into sleep. I knew he probably would not remember this crystalline moment, but that didn't seem to matter.

***

My father has a peculiar place in my heart. I know he loved me. I also know he never *knew* me, and never came to know our kids. Andrew, the middle child, always felt an attachment to his grandpa. Just after he died, Andrew found a photo and frame, and propped his grandfather's picture on his bureau. Discovering it brought tears to my eyes. The only other tears I shed was when I told our youngest, and we both cried. My emotional connection with my father seems to circuit through my own children. What do I make of this?

There is a moment barely two years after his death that I remember and hold dear. This was rare: a day spent at home, one child and me alone, variously engaged. Andrew had just graduated from high school and was preparing for a move to Alberta to find work in the oil patch (a move which thrilled him, while terrifying us). Wading through an accumulation of stuff in his room, he had discovered his baby book.

He found me at the ironing board and read me the phrases that had caught his attention: *Woke up on his sixth day and cried for twelve straight weeks.... Such long fingers and toes!*

"This is *sweet!*" he exclaimed, laughing. While I knew that "sweet" signified something different to him, it felt good that he was touched by this condensed record of his infancy.

And yes, that memory *was* sweet, as was this moment. They converge to create a telescopic sensation, typical of memories. After becoming so accustomed to the state of forgetfulness, being so wholly able to remember—a state for which we seem to lack a word—is an indulgence.

Click: It's eighteen years ago. The image of that baby in my arms is as real as the sight of this lanky, long-haired, broad-shouldered boy in front of me. If memory *didn't* lapse, then maybe the sweetness of these moments would be so much diminished. And yet...

***

The summer after my dad died, I read Bill Bryson's book, *A Short History of Nearly Everything*. I loved it: read greedily, wholly enthralled, delighting in Bryson's far-ranging curiosity, his humour, his zeal for all that is quirky. Yet I knew, even as I made my way through successive chapters, that I was losing the rich detail of chapters that came before. Surely I would distill *something* of value to keep hold of, but could neither anticipate, nor control, what it might be.

It's been years now. I don't forget the pleasure of reading this book. I remember the broad sweep of Bryson's perspective; that life is precarious and the universe amazing, and that we are probably never going to be capable of comprehending its magnitude or essence. Sometimes, a single fact will surface—a random detail about a bug or fish, or a cloud formation.

Once, on a southbound flight from Calgary, the pilot announced that we could glimpse Yellowstone National Park from the left of the plane. His announcement prompted this crushing sense of doom which arose from some residual shred of memory from Bryson's book. A spasm of fear, with no attendant context, left as suddenly as it had come. And this fleeting sensation, against all odds, I remember.

TEENS IN THE FAMILY

The house is full of teens, so disruptive to normal routine, to the elemental rhythm of day and night. Last night they roamed the house for hours after my husband and I drifted off to sleep—him, falling into the fast and fitful rest of the physically beat; me gliding gently from the pages of my book into the restless sleep of the menopausal. The kids are still going strong at three a.m.; we get up before seven. I hear the murmur of television, the low baseline thrum of some song. Toilets flush. Cupboards close and dishes clatter. A golden cone of light streams in under our bedroom door. Resigned to wakefulness, I try to gauge the moods, hoping for light amiability and wishing for silence and darkness. Wishing for sleeping children and a house at rest.

The teens are disruptive of nearly every aspect of home-life, and I have trouble finding my way among them. And yet I feel as lost when they are away from here as when they're all here. I should have expected teen years to be this way. But like everything else in this evolving family life, it's surprised me.

We are navigating a house of moods. Every day, any moment, a new mood will erupt, a crisis materializing from thin air and dust. Caring for infants was taxing, and toddlers were exhausting, but all the hype about teens turns out to have been understated. I want to know when—or how, or even just *if*—we will all emerge from this stage, intact: still a family.

***

It's a high wire act, and if there were a net, we never get around to putting it up.

Walking the wire, holding that unwieldy pole, we try to balance between wisdom and ignorance, between instinct and principles. And maybe they do the same. Who knows? I really only know what it's like for me, as our children, one after the other, have entered their teen years. Every now and then, I feel a blow to the gut—circumstances shift just so, leaving me knocked off balance. At other times, it feels all but impossible just to keep going.

***

Perspective shifts from my kids to myself as a kid and, as trite as it seems, I am so sorry for my mother. What felt utterly isolating to me—my own *private* turmoil—was, I now know, absolutely connecting us through the umbilical cord of acuity. My quest for comfort in the music of Simon and Garfunkel... my solitary habits—long runs and long spells of reading... my need for independence, which took me to Montana and beyond.... even the intensity of my studying, with a focus barely distinct from obsession... What could that have been like for her?

***

Teens fall off the high wire, and this I do know. I can remember tumbling headlong; the verge of panic, the disorientation and, sometimes, a despondency so dark I was certain I'd never move though it to another side; never know light again. Twenty-five years later, I've watched my daughter do the same, not a bit less helpless watching now than when it was me falling. I believe she will be fine, which should make it easier. But I also remember how scary it feels, and how it hurts. And through it all, how distant the parents seem.

Sometimes a teen will manage to grab hold as she falls, grasping by the fingertips. The kid will restore the balance in a move as unexpected as the fall, a grace of serendipity and goodwill. As simple as this: the eruption of words, blowing us apart at dinner; alarm turning the stomach hard; fear of irreparable damage done by words flung one to the other. It's the middle kid this time, the one whose attitude rises to overcome even himself. Twenty minutes. Hard minutes—stone-hard, punctuated by the slam of a door. Then he's back, throwing himself on the couch to watch the dumb movie we share.

Or this. The day I issue ultimatums, and we don't speak for one day, two days. Gestures thrown like javelins over breakfast cereal, the sameness of the routine driving home the strangeness of mood. Then a day of laughter, and small healing gestures. And simple as that, we are back on the high wire. Never quite at ease, but slip-sliding along.

There are those forty-five-minute drives home from school, or the soccer field, or music lessons, when the silence is so thick that I could grab a handful and squeeze it, reducing it to some stony extract which will divulge no more than the child who sits beside me. I wrack my brain for explanations: What was last said? Who offended whom? Is this guilt, or rage, or unspeakable despair? Does it have *anything* to do with me?

How does it happen that toddlers—who would chatter with such vibrancy and stamina that sometimes I was certain my head would explode with the effort of listening—become teens capable of passing whole hours uttering only strangulated syllables in answers to my stream of questions? What can it mean when our sixteen-year-old emerges from his room with the greeting "Word"—barely a vowel sounding to hold together the three consonants, lips immobile, face not registering so much as a flicker of expression? My instinct registers a muted cordiality. I suspect that to him, this is high sophistication: communication stripped down to its optimum simplicity. To me, its regression, falling short of primate levels of primitive. I find myself longing for that mind-numbing chatter of a dozen years ago.

Our youngest, at twelve, provides spells of relief. Yet he's so obviously teetering between being sweet and eager for companionship, and as rife with attitude as either of the older two—both of whom he watches, as though studying for an exam. He'll converse with me in the hours we spend together, both of us deserted by the increasingly busy lives of the older two. He's interesting and engaging—actually registers emotions and responds to them. But he is drawn to his sister and brother, already trying out the inarticulate syllabic response to our questions, when he remembers. And, being both a very social child and at that most social phase of pre-teenhood, he is drawn—more drawn, in fact, than either of his siblings were—to his peers.

***

Oh the peers! They exert such a pull away from us, from the heart of family. They are positively seductive and they beckon by phone, or screen, or school bus. Their allure is, I suspect, their distinctiveness from us (the hopelessly boring and familiar). So by default, they will be what we have strived *not* to be: rootless, haphazard, unclean; maybe even unsafe. Their parents will counter home baking with processed cheese spread; home built rural with trailer park; cautious middle-age with youthful indifference.

Home becomes, for a teenager, a state of restriction; freedom becoming, then, a place away from home. Yet for me, home remains the ideal, and I find myself longing for those occasions when all five of us are there together, most always with an uncle and nowadays, usually a friend or two. I love when we are sharing a single topic of conversation, something as mundane as the pasta we eat, the rain or lack of it, some sport or other. For me, this is the best of what life will serve up: intimacy, safety, stability. It *must* be the whole point of all this other, the work and strife. It's a joy that has become as rare as it is lovely.

Looming to dispel the joy of these gatherings is the awareness that—even as we become more adept at navigating the tensions of our own high wire act, managing the inevitable conflicts that percolate—the opportunity to gather, with its attendant challenges of proximity, becomes ever more precious. Teens grow up and pull away. And while we long for a life of serenity and focus which they make so impossible, the idea of their leaving fills me with despair.

***

Two stories take me to that eventuality.

One evening I was asking another mom—a friend with whom I've shared an accumulation of hours standing on the sidelines of soccer fields—how it felt having her youngest son move out of town to live with his dad. She and her husband had split up in the past year, and I'd thought that her son's choice could have been seen as an act of desertion, and hurtful. She said no; it was more about this boy wanting to be at the lake, and with his dad, rather than *not* being with her. But she said it does hurt, not having all of her chicks roosting in one spot. This surprised me, maybe because her oldest chick was twenty-five.

It was the very next morning, on my way to work, when I veered out toward the shoulder of the highway. From the corner of my eye, I'd spotted a duck making her way, in a stately and unhurried fashion, across four busy lanes of traffic. Then I noticed that she led a procession of ducklings: her five offspring making their way, oblivious to all but the one duck in front of them, connected by a strand of trust and instinct to Mom, as she navigated majestically across the highway. I remember watching over my shoulder even as I navigated my own way through the streams of traffic flowing up Highway 5 toward the Trans-Canada East, to see her clear lane after lane, and feeling relief for that.

Thoughts of her trailed through my mind for days. What impressed me were her blindness to the danger, and her oblivion to all but her mission of leading the little ones across the road. Maybe, though, she was impelled by, rather than blind to, the sense of danger. Perhaps alone she would have hustled, but her maternal instinct restrained her to the dignified pageantry of leading her charges. Who can know?

What I do know is that these two images—of my friend's chicks roosting in one cluster, and of that mother duck's voyage of dumb-luck or blind grace—resonate with me. I imagine missing the kids, as I progress through the less engaging tasks of the morning: prying ice-cream bowls from the countertop to wedge into the dishwasher; shaking out the jeans heaped in a corner (complete with boxers, smelly socks still in pant-legs, as though the kid had ejected from the outfit, right there in the living room); puzzling over how to hang up a thong, so spare that no part quite engages the grip of clothespin.

Late mornings at home are when I feel, most keenly, the temptation to let go gracefully, to embrace a sense of solitude and ease which may have been part of life before children. From the biological perspective, I suppose these kids are working hard at making themselves unappealing, unlovable even, so that their eventual departures will not break our hearts. I'd like to tell them to ease off a bit, that we are making good progress toward that eventual release. But then I think of my friend's comment on the soccer field, and I know that—even though I feel ready—deep down, despite the risks and the bedlam, I still want all my ducks in that row.

TOGETHER OR APART?

i) The Question

When our kids were small, they invented this riddle that they found riotously funny, a joke with staying power far exceeding its ingenuity.

Iterations went like this: One would push his plate toward the other, with a pancake torn in two, and pushed together—or pieces of toast welded with peach jam, or apple slices mashed together—and ask, "Is it together, or apart?"

Together, or apart?

The expected answer was *always* "together," and the correct answer, always, of course, "Apart!!!" That was it. And while many details of life escape the slackening grip of memory, I never forget this stupid riddle. It comes to me at the most absurd times, and every time has the power to make me laugh. Such is unfathomable power of life in the family.

ii) Said and Unsaid

Date: 2/21, 3:09 PM
To: Nina
Subject: Back in Kamloops

> So, Dad and I made it to someplace between Spence's Bridge and Lytton—waited behind some major accident for maybe an hour, then turned back. We heard it could have been a 12 hour wait!! Anyway, just booked a flight and am still staying till Sun. morning...
>
> Hoping to see you tomorrow for dinner. ... Too bad our plans didn't work, and Dad misses being there too. Aughh.... Can't say we didn't try!
> Soon, Mom

Date: 2/21, 10:32 PM
To: Nina
Subject: from hotel room, Van.

> Hey Hon,
> Just got out of the meetings—eating room service—sooo hungry. Quite the day!
>
> Cindy and I present tomorrow (twice, AM & PM), so will probably go down for an early breakfast. If you're awake before, say, 7:45, give me a call. But if you're not up, don't worry. We should be done by 4, I think...
>
> A bit scattered still from the rushed night. I'd better eat, shower, and review presentation notes. Will be so good to see you tomorrow.
> xo mom

Date: 2/21, 10:56 PM
To: Mont
Subject: from Van.

> Hey,
> Just eating a room service smoothie and soup. Found my way here from train station fine, threw stuff in the room and got to our meeting 15 mins late. What a day, eh? Hope you scrounged up a decent dinner.
> I miss you being here. Not nearly so much fun w/o you.

Date: 2/22, 8:00 AM
To: Nina
Subject: new day

> Morning Hon,
> Up early for some gym time and a shower (YES!!) and feeling lots, *lots* better.
>
> Off for pre-conf breakfast. Hope to hear from—or see you—soon!
>
> Idea! You could meet me at the wine & cheese afterwards—between 3 and 4:00, 34th floor. I'll come back at lunch and see if you've responded to that. Would keep an eye out for you (but am hard to miss—generally at outer edges of the action).
>
> OR, whenever you want to meet is good. Am surprisingly rested after a fairly short sleep. Even feeling ready to present.
> see you soon, mom

Date: 2/22, 8:01 AM
To: Mont
Subject: new day

> Got a Saturday *Globe*! Up early, quick workout, and feeling pretty good, despite not much sleep. Used my iPod at the gym—just like a city person. Cold and grey out.
>
> See you tomorrow. Will be in touch. Wish us luck w/ the presentations...
> xo me

Date: 2/22, 12:01 PM
To: Nina
Subject: hoping to hear from you...

> Hey Hon,
> So, come to our wine & cheese for sure, if you don't mind and can get here before 4—but on 2nd floor, not 34 (where we're presenting, not wine/cheesing). Either walk up or press 2 on the keypad by the elevators, and it will tell you which elevator.
>
> If I don't see you there, I'll expect you here later, so no pressure.
> see you soon!!
> PS it's all going fine... One presentation down/one to go...
> xo m

Date: 2/22, 11:28 PM
To: Cindy
Subject: update (back at hotel)

>Hi,
>Just back now.
>She got out of surgery about 10—appendectomy —
>JUST in time. So scary, and a long, long day. A good
>hospital though. Got to change my flight to a later one
>so I can see her in recovery.
>
>To add insult to injury, she passed out on her way
>back from an ultrasound, and broke a tooth.
>
>So very glad I was here though. That's the blessing.
>See you next week. And yes, I thought our
>presentations went well, too. PS *Still* snowing!!
>-e

Date: 2/22, 11:55 PM
To: Mont
Subject: changing flight home

>Hey,
>That was about as easy as it was to book the flight
>here, in my office yesterday—same slow, strange
>loop, thinking it hadn't worked, but then it *maybe*
>did...
>
>Feels better to wait it out, so I'll extend my room a
>night, and hang in there (plus catch up sleep, etc.).
>Strange couple days, eh?
>See you Mon. and talk to you tomorrow.
>xo me

Date: 2/23, 7:30 AM
To: James, Andrew
Subject: your sister

Hey Guys,
Just off the phone w/ Dad—a quick email for now...
Ryan took Nina to emerg. yesterday at 3AM w/ stomach pains. He called me from VGH at 3PM when we were supposed to be meeting up to have dinner... She had appendicitis. Short version of a long story— surgery last night at 8—out by maybe 9:30. Ryan and I left hospital maybe 11... him to search for cab for me.

Just finally really awake again and on my way back to hospital. Changed flight—till tomorrow. Got to find something to eat (been a while—nothing available last night by when I got back here). Poor N—long, rough day. She passed out in emerg. hospital and broke a tooth—as if this all weren't enough. Turns out the surgery went fine—they were able to go laparoscopic. But they said it was the last possible hour or it would've gone septic or something.

Nina was almost Ry's colour when I saw her. And he was even, if possible, more pale than usual.

Long other story why I flew, and was here alone— otherwise, Dad & I would both have been here enjoying a couple days w/ N&R...

Call Dad for updates. I'll call him from hospital once we know how things are going.

Hope you guys are good. Cool thing: Horns filled the streets in the middle of my sleep. Gold! So exciting and positive and not quite what I was expecting to wake up to...Am off to the hospital now (hoping to find it once again)...

xo Mom
from Hotel

Date: 2/23, 8:45 PM
To: Mont
Subject: update from Van.

Hi,
Am back in my room for tonight.
Nina's looking better--more like herself. Still quite sore and tender, of course, but her colour is coming back, and she's alert, even ate a few bites. Ryan finished off the lousy hospital dinner.

Am a pro at getting to and from the train now. Going to get a good sleep, go to the gym maybe, and be back at VGH for start of visiting at 9.

Lots of time to get back to the airport so nice it's not till 1 PM. See you tomorrow. Call tonight if you happen to get this, or through the kids' phones after 9--or see you by 2.
xo me

Date: 2/24, 1:00 AM
To: James
Subject: from Van.

> Hey Hon,
> Thanks for popping that episode of *Girls* in Dropbox for me—watched it tonight to wind down to get a good sleep.
>
> Nina's much better, though still pretty wiped, and uncomfortable. But she'll be able to go home tomorrow, probably even while I'm there in the morning.
>
> They're both okay. We spent lots of time hanging out in Nina's hospital room, and she was even alert and awake for most of this afternoon.
>
> I'm flying home at 1PM. Hope you have a good Monday.
> xo mom

Date: 2/24, 10:15 AM
To: Mont
Subject: from N & R's!

> Hey,
> Ryan called me this morning to say Nicole was good to go home.
>
> So she left VGH around 9, and I came here instead. She's doing fine. Ry's out getting us bagels.
>
> Am watching flight updates (still snowing like crazy out there). Will call if I'm delayed. All morning flights

were held up an hr. each. So don't leave too early to get me.

See you soon.
xo me

Date: 2/24, 1:47 PM
To: Nina
Subject: from Airport

Hey Hon,
So, well—I *missed* my flight. By maybe as little as 3-4 minutes.

Spent an hr. rebooking—first time I can get out is 7AM. Should have said to make it 10:45 but not thinking fast or well. Feel really dumb...

Am thinking I should just find a comfortable spot and stay here.

Really, really not wanting to I intrude—so just checking on what you think about me making my way back to take up your couch tonight. Would set up a cab to get me at 5 or so.

You've got friends coming, right? Would it be kind of weird to have me in the middle? I can stick around here for a while easily. And really don't mind just staying here.

Let me know what you think.
xo mom

Date: 2/24, 1:53 PM
To: James
Subject: from airport

> So… to add one more chapter to this long, complicated weekend, I missed my flight (by minutes—was here by 12:20 for a 1:00. Snow held up the transit. ARGGGHHH…) Am feeling weird about going back to Nina's w/ them adjusting now to her being home. But likely will…
>
> Will call later tomorrow. Hope you're good. We knew you'd be stoked from the games. Nina is mending fine—was really lucky to get that surgery when she did, I think. Pretty scary, but by 10PM, it was all okay. She was happy to get messages from you and Andrew.
>
> Would help if it would stop snowing—my glasses are perpetually covered w/ snow. Feet damp and cold for so long they might never be warm. May have to run a laundry tonight (have worn the same clothes for pretty much 3 days). Anyway, good to "chat" in this weird in-between space.
> xo mom

Date: 2/24, 2:17 PM
To: Nina
Subject: RE: from Airport

> Thanks Hon!
> At least I know the way to your place now.
> So two quick questions: If I do want to bus closer (if the snow's still on the sidewalk I MIGHT) which bus # again, and where do I get off?

And, there's a little market here I'll walk by. Want anything—at all? No whim too minor. I'm not in any rush *now*...
PS the train had an emergency hold up which is likely where I lost those few minutes.
xo me

Date: 2/24, 2:20 PM
To: Mont
Subject: from Van AP

Connected w N & R. All's good... Heading back in a bit.

Will arrange a cab to pick me up there at 5 AM, and see you by 8-ish. Again, though, decent chance of delays. Could cab from AP to work if you want to come get me after work instead....
xo me

Date: 2/24, 2:27 PM
To: Nina
Subject: RE: RE: from Airport

Thanks for the bus info...
See you in a while. Not rushing, so enjoy your space till I get there....
mom

Date: 2/24, 5:01 PM
To: Vancouver Taxi
Subject: early pick up for 2/25

>Thanks very much.
>It's a basement apartment, but I'll watch from the window before and be outside at 5:30. After missing a flight today, I want to be sure to be there by or at 6 AM.

>See you in the morning.
>Best,
>E...

Date: 2/24, 5:05 PM
To: Mont
Subject: back at N & R's

>Hey,
>I'm back here now. Just going for a walk to maybe check out this chowder place Nina told us about. Feeling better about it all, now. Have a cab lined up for 5:30, so all good.

>Can you bring me some clean clothes? My tan cords with the navy & white flannel shirt plus a pair of underwear would be just great—comfortable, *and* clean. Didn't bother running laundry. Nina's resting, and they have friends bringing Chinese take-out I picked out a bit better than usual wine (I hope, anyway), which I'll leave for when Nina's up to it.

>See you in the morning. Sucks you have to come back to town to get me... Will be good to see you, though.
>xo me

Date: 2/25, 9:15 AM
To: Nina
Subject: from office

Hey Hon,
Tried twice to send you emails from the AP—but they didn't send.. Strange. Wondering now what else I sent didn't go out(??)... Oh well.

Thanks for last night. The couch was quite comfortable. Jean Luc was hugely entertaining from his "office"/jail cell but didn't disturb my rest. I didn't actually sleep much, but rested well (too beat even to read). Had one crazy nightmare—so real—that it was almost 6 and I'd missed cab *and* flight. It was maybe 4:40 though, so I just got up. Hope you guys got some rest.

Cabbie was in good time. I released JL from confinement. He didn't manage to escape—and the outside cat never got in either (that I noticed). I did leave the door unlocked though.

Hope you're feeling still better today.
Love you, Mom...

iii) Small Blessings

We had room to turn around on the narrow, twisting Canyon Highway. The trucker behind us didn't, he explained to my husband when he shared what he knew of the accident ahead.

I was able to book a flight with not an hour to spare.

I would be back in my room at 3:05 PM, between presentation and reception, the moment Ryan would call from the parking lot of Emergency.

Someone noticed the broken-off piece of my daughter's front tooth after she'd passed out on the floor of the exam room.

Back in my room that night *I discovered an orange carried away from our meeting* the night before, a nail file with which to pierce its thick skin.

Canadian men won Gold! And I would know this the moment it happened, when the cheers erupted from the streets, eleven floors below.

Stuffed in my pocket was a toque and gloves. I was never lost for more than five minutes or turned around by more than one city block.

iv) Pulling Together

On the flight back home, I recorded notes, as if I might forget the chill of wearing damp jeans, the glasses fogged to opaque, nose and eyes perpetually dripping; or the beauty of falling snow, melting as it hit the streets, eerily still on that Sunday night. But I *had* forgotten that one bit— those empty, glistening streets. And honestly, I'd forgotten the dampness too. And even the sharp edges of anxiety in the uncertainty of what was wrong with my daughter, the raw fear of her boyfriend, the terrifying efficiency of the emergency ward.

I want to remember, though; am thankful for all the reminders. Because fear, and the blessing of surviving it, and the webs of connection—to family, to friends, to kind and indifferent strangers—make life more than a succession of bland hours, of ordinary days. It's where I find the outlines of what matters.

v) Full Circles

We were in the North Bay Pre-Op wing: the inner sanctum. I took care to keep out of the way in a place with little capacity other than for the business at hand. Around us, incredibly young people moved with competence and even a kind of grace, performing their interlinked and intricate jobs. Amid the coded communication of that work, they also conveyed whatever news of the Gold Medal game that leaked from lounges or recovery room TVs. More drama folded into the peculiar mix of tension and crazy-making long waits.

There in Pre-Op, I stood beside my daughter, trying to hold myself together; trying not to see or hear anything that might make me faint. My job was to keep her company, to reassure, and to distract her from the cries of the patient in an opposite bay. In those moments when she gave way to the drugs and the hunger, dropping into a daze, I'd find my eyes drawn to the heart monitor, locking into its rhythm as if *my* life depended on it. It was like a hypnotic trance. Or a ledge I'd surely fall from, even at the possibility that the pattern would be interrupted; that any single edge-dip-rise might swoop crazily off. I knew, with certainty, that I'd been in this place before. When?

And then I remember. This was another hospital, with *me* strapped to the monitor, left to wait for a drug to induce labour for a pregnancy that had resisted completion. The heartbeat I watched, as if everything I knew depended upon my vigilance, was of this child (then a day from her birth; now, at twenty-eight, a child only to her dad and me).

And now, I was *so* excited to tell her this coincidence, to share this story. But she was fast asleep, long and lovely, her breathing regular, her bare feet pushing up and down to some persistent urge toward wakefulness. Her face was pale, eyes closed with shadows etched below the lashes. And that heartbeat, thumping on.

Together, I thought to myself: We are *together*.

COOKIES ARE A KIND OF LOVE

Had it not been for changes in our family life, I might never have realized how my feelings for family are manifest in the simplest acts of stirring and scooping and shaping of batter. It might never have occurred to me to consider the act of preparing food—of baking cookies or rolling pie crust, of chopping celery or building lasagne—as an expression of love.

***

Our daughter turned thirty last year. Before her second birthday, she had firmly asserted herself as vegetarian. I responded by getting serious about making cookies. She was small for her age, but strong-minded about what she liked and did not like. The Do-Not-Like list was growing, and by then included meat, chicken, fish, eggs, and cheese.

We tried to entice her to expand her tastes. One week, convinced that her diminishing palate was a consequence of my long workdays—of our failure to sit together for dinner—I redoubled my efforts on that front. Ensconced in her clip-on denim chair, she seemed content situated between us at the table. We still remember how she turned to ask, "Could you move your plate, Daddy? The 'snell' gets in my nose." It was a relief to settle back into our more comfortable routine: our daughter happily snacking, a cup of milk, some noodles or rice and leftover veggies in front of her; her seat clamped onto the counter in its usual position—opposite where I prepared the meal her dad and I would eat later, often after she'd gone to bed.

Another strategy, maybe more successful—more enduring, for certain—was baking our cookies. Making cookies was one way to ensure that she got a bit of protein and other good stuff: whole wheat and wheat germ or oats sifted into the dry ingredients; fresh eggs, and real butter rather than some suspect oil-based product. Into most batters I stirred raisins and nuts or seeds. Soon, I was supplementing the mix with ground nuts and soy or bean flour.

Our daughter liked baking, and I most always involved her. At first, she'd be put off by the eggs and butter, being fond of neither. I'd furtively blend those first ingredients before she'd noticed. Mixed with brown sugar, they resembled peanut butter, which she loved. Her jobs were sifting dry ingredients—done with relish (clouds of flour rising around her); stirring before the batter became too hard going; dumping in scoopfuls of chocolate chips or nuts or raisins; and helping to shape the cookies. She especially enjoyed pressing the balls of batter with a fork. After the first of her younger brothers had come along, whenever things verged on frantic and she needed distracting, I'd pour oats and maybe cinnamon and raisins into a bowl and give her the pastry blender. A blending job never failed to keep her busy and entertained. It would work for her brothers, too, their flour clouds escalating toward tornado magnitude.

Across a span of thirty-some years, on most Sundays I've baked cookies or squares, often triple batches, filling cans or blue-lidded plastic peanut butter jars to stack in the freezer. By even a conservative estimate I have made approximately 5800 dozen cookies, not including the pan of brownies baked early this morning.

***

Our standards include peanut butter-chocolate chip or oatmeal (with raisins and coconut). Snicker doodles were new to me, but how to resist the name? My recipe may have been the single positive outcome from those terrible low-fat-diet days. A preponderance of egg white gives them their pale colour and tender chewiness; cinnamon lends a trail of fragrance. Our Special K cookie recipe is cut from a cereal box. Monkey faces came directly from my childhood by way of an inherited recipe. Mine feature the heavy hand of whole wheat and flaxseed, and enough ginger to make the eyes water. Our brownies derive from a recipe meticulously handwritten in thick pencil by a teammate from our younger son's 12-and-under soccer days. (He would not be responsible for the portion of bean flour featured in my version.)

Christmastime shifts the repertoire. The standbys, eternally rotated the rest of the year, give way to the decadence of butter tarts (thanks to a *Harrowsmith* recipe tweaked to resemble my husband's grandmother's famous Black Currant Tarts: less butter, *loads* of currants). Snowballs are my concession to decadence—to the festive craving for shortbread (code for white flour and butter). Betty Crocker's candy cane cookies, straight from the

1950's via a mimeographed recipe, also descend from shortbread. Though I use butter, the recipe calls for shortening, and the even more dubious red food-colouring. Rolling and twisting the cords of soft dough requires colossal patience (which my mother definitely did *not* have—and yet, she made them by the dozens).

More recently, we—or more accurately, my daughter, with a kitchen full of useless bystanders—made *pizzelles*, pressing them one by one until they're the perfect, slightly golden state of doneness, their vanilla or anise or almond fragrance spilling out from the seams of the press.

***

Most Sundays unfold to a routine I cherish. They begin with a cappuccino and the breakfast my husband makes for me: an egg soft-cooked in a toast hole (replicating one made by the mother in the movie *Moonstruck*, on the morning that all hell broke loose). Another coffee, a few sections of the Saturday *Globe & Mail*, and a load of laundry follow in no particular order, giving way to a round of baking or cooking, and a long run or ski or hike. The leisurely nature of that procession supplants the anything-but-leisurely pace of Sundays when the kids were young, each needing to be at some field or rink to play one sport or other. (Oddly, we sometimes find ourselves missing that other, more frantic version of Sunday.)

On a good weekend—then as now—by Sunday dinner a pot of soup or stew or a casserole will sit cooling, in the ready for a weekday dinner; clean laundry folded in stacks on the staircase; and a couple dozen cookies safely stashed in the freezer (another dozen typically polished off by flow-through traffic). In late summer there might be seven quart-sealers of peaches cooling on a tea towel. My regular workweek, as engaging as it tends to be, can't touch a Sunday evening for that sweet sense of fulfilment.

***

As the two boys grew older, the quantity and pace of production increased to meet the surging appetites of previously unimaginable capacity. The boys followed their sister by three and seven years; but she started us off so gently, eating like a bird—albeit a very particular, vegetarian bird. All three kids were—still are—active. They've grown to love eating well and cooking, too. Our social life was—is still—fairly simple, being fundamentally comprised of the preparing and sharing of meals. Our traditions revolve around special foods, generally carnivorous-friendly in nature: for Easter, ham (at its best from our own pork; cured by our own butcher); for Thanksgiving and Christmas, stuffed and roasted turkey; for birthdays, the choice rests with the star of the day (plus a side of meat to appease the boys, if it's their sister's day).

Although in other respects exceedingly far from formal, we did manage to share many of those meals crowded around the dining room table—a scarred and stained oaken oval that made its way from my childhood home in Maine.

***

The ordinary shape of family, despite our utter inattentiveness to it, changes. And we adjust, transforming our ways.

First one child and then the next left for university. When someone would be going to visit or mailing a parcel, they'd always be happy to get cookies from home. A jar or two of peach jam would never be refused. Our daughter usually would return home bearing containers and jars; her brothers, never.

***

Across the years, as we were re-learning what to do with our time, travel and maturity were nudging the kids toward more adventurous attitudes toward eating. Our collective tastes grew more sophisticated. On those occasions—by now regarded as exceptional—when we would all five be home, a favourite family undertaking would be to prepare a meal of tacos—with colourful heaps of condiments in bowls of every size; or lettuce wraps— folded around prawns, or shaved carrot and peanuts, or marinated chicken slices.

A bit of serendipity involving an evening teaching assignment taken on at this juncture transferred the day-to-day dinner responsibility to my husband. He assumed the role with pluck which grew to panache. It slipped from my shoulders so easily; I've never taken it back.

Where I'd grown cautious and predictable over the years, worn down by kids' equivocating tastes and proclivity for protest, he is daring, a culinary adventurer. *Chili rellanos*? No problem. We have *two* versions. Home-made tacos shells? Elementary! The evening meal, once a routine centrepiece to the rambunctious drawing together of the day, now serves as a gastronomic event.

In the more recent years that followed the third university graduation, we'd continue to reunite around our kitchen to try a new dish, or to elaborate on an old one. One December, our daughter coached us through hand rolling pasta; the summer before, her younger brother had guided us through crafting wontons, his girlfriend patiently steaming and frying our variously shaped savoury packets. The year before, it was the older brother showing me how to properly finish risotto (a skill mastered that summer he washed pots for a local restaurant). Less a lesson than a benign take-over, he shouldered me aside, impatient with my ineffectual fussing. He cranked up the flame, stirring in handful of grated parmesan with vigour; in minutes, we had buttery-smooth, perfect risotto. Its perfection was a surprise (so too, the confidence, the muscled arms—all characterising a man—not the boy I still expect him to be).

***

Those stories, dipped from the kids' earliest years, garnished with a sprinkling from the most recent years, bracket a time and a change that rocked us. This is the one I've let memory sweep around, the story my account has skirted. But this is what pulled me into these meditations on food and family, and here I will go.

***

In these years, the older two were away in university and beyond. At home, we were three: our youngest adrift in his later teens.

Each day required a brave attempt to begin on a bright note. Inevitably, the moment would come when my stomach would clench as I watched the finely articulated jawbones of our youngest son work, chewing, chewing. I could see the veins in his neck, the texture of muscle along his upper arms, the curve of the bone hollowing out around those shadowed eyes which looked too round for his angular face. On the occasions when I'd venture a hug or pat his back as he leaned from his stool, I'd be shocked by the fragile feel of his shoulder blades. They'd jut out at an impossible extent, with the heft of a sparrow's wing.

***

What was this thing with its tentacles wrapped around our child? How could we wrestle it to the ground without injuring the frail individual within its clutches? Frail: not how I'd *ever* have imagined describing this boy. Always small for his age, he was a bundle of energy: strong, supple, irrepressible. He was the kid on the soccer team who'd put down, heaven knows where, a *monster* breakfast—three eggs, toast, bacon, hash browns with ketchup—with room for an apple afterwards. A robust athlete; a champion eater.

And then? Some meals, he could not bring himself to sit with us. He'd fuss about the kitchen, tidying up the counter, putting things away, serving us. Any probing questions about eating or *not* eating, any hint that his hovering was making us uneasy, would send him fleeing.

On a good day, or hour, we'd keep those comments to ourselves, prattling on about anything that seemed safe, any frivolous food- and tension-free topic, to get through our meal.

It was even harder, perversely, on those longed-for occasions when his siblings would return home. Meals when he *would* sit with us, the effort not to watch him was its own form of torture: not watching as he served himself a tiny portion of meat, greens from the salad bowl before they got tossed with dressing, the smallest boiled new potatoes. We'd avert our gaze so as not to notice as he sorted his half of boneless, skinless chicken breast into two piles of shreds, slowly eating his way through one; scraping the other into the dog dish the second he finished. Hard as we worked not to look, it was impossible not to see. His brother would shovel down quantities that seemed shocking by contrast, almost as an antidote. Once, they would have challenged one another for the biggest turkey leg, laughing as they competed for seconds. Now, one brother protected the other by distracting us with inane chatter, modeling whatever normal is.

Another day I remember like it's yesterday: He's sitting for dinner, shifting uneasily in his chair, picking at plain salad greens and an impossibly small mound of pasta, working with his fork to separate the ground beef out of the meat sauce—not long ago his favourite part. An eternity later, another ordeal of dinner is done. An hour later and he sits, alone, back at the table, eating a bowl of Cheerios—with milk even. And then another. And another. Inside I'm reeling with relief, with joy; outside, implacable. Half hour more and he's on the couch squirming with pain. Try to relax, I urge, to let the body get used to the feeling of fullness. Oats are gentle, I add. Try to let them settle. Another hour passes and I think I hear him retching in the bathroom downstairs.

***

Surely love changes us, and this too changed us. Changed me. By nature fairly optimistic and cheerful, hardly a single day passed with no tears. They'd leak at the most disconcerting times, sometimes squeezing out and running onto the pillow as I practised sleep. I remember wondering how there could be any more tears; how my cheeks hadn't eroded from their briny flow.

***

Looking back at this recollection, the anxiety, rebounding, bruises me. I still don't know anything, I realize. I've oversimplified all of it. We never had a clue how to give him whatever he needed to get through this. But miraculously, we are a family who would get to the other side of this. And be stronger for having travelled through it. But the ordeal was not done with us yet.

***

My journal holds this account of one summer day. The older brother is home for a summer job, and on this day they're off with their dad to see a Lion's game in Vancouver. The house is mine. I have biked, gardened, changed beds, and done laundry. Bread is baking, a pitcher of iced tea is steeping, and cabbage stew simmers on the stove. This is my writing time—less and later than I'd hoped, but with the golden sun of dusk streaming in the front windows, and the smell of bread baking. Except that I am utterly drained.

Earlier, I'd been upstairs pulling sheets from beds in the kids' rooms. Pushing the frame back to the wall, I found my son's soccer bag wedged in behind the bed, feeling heavy. With an equally heavy heart, I drew in a breath and unzipped the duffel. Inside were grocery bags, their handles tightly knotted. In one were tomato sauce jars, a wild-berry jam jar, a bottle of barbeque sauce—all empty, with lids screwed tightly on. One jar had mould inside. There was an empty chip bag, with cracker and cookie boxes rolled up inside, one of those in turn stuffed with banana peels. In the side pocket of the duffel, a full package of cheap wieners wrapped in plastic was date-stamped for a month past.

I was stunned. In the wake of shock came panic: My god, he will poison himself, I thought. What levels of nervousness, shame, misery, craving would have driven him to hoard food, and then to hide the evidence? Beyond the waves of fear and sadness, uncertainty: What should I do? What could I do? I was alone with this: How could I tell my husband? He'd be devastated. It would only extend the sadness and worry from me to him.

What I did, finally, was to take all of it downstairs, sorting it, rinsing what could be recycled; discarding the rest. I'd emptied the trash from every room, so that the bags would be discreetly stashed amid others. There was no escaping the truth: I was now complicit, having surrendered to the compulsion to hide this affliction. Finally, I sat to write a note, telling him that I was sorry to have invaded his privacy. Asking him not to be mad—or embarrassed. Suggesting that it might seem reasonable to hoard after months of what must have felt like starvation. Suggesting, once again, getting help (real help, and not our bungling, well-meaning version of it).

I resisted the impulse to stop laying down words, and then battled the urge to crumble the note. Instead, I folded the page carefully and placed it—alongside a fresh package of saltines—in the duffle, now nearly as hollow as I felt.

Then, feeling bereft, I pulled myself onto my bicycle to ride it all away. I flew the five kilometres downhill to the second cattle-guard. Despite the long haul back to the house, one minute I was dreading the steepest part, and the next, at the end of our laneway. I'd peddled up that hill without even dropping into a lower gear, which would kill me on a normal day. It was as if the day had left me stronger. Emotionally too, I hoped. But what good, I wrote, was all that strength when I had neither courage nor wisdom from which to act?

That's where my account left off, trailing into a few more mundane details of the day. But there *was* one more thing I noticed: Finding these stashes (it would happen again), would make me feel sick. And yet, afterwards, I'd have this urge to eat. That first time, I ate two slices of bread with peanut butter, and then handfuls of corn chips, a banana, and a glass of milk. It may not sound like much, item by item, but the accumulation left me feeling heavy, and yes, like a flashback to my own adolescent eating compulsions. I still notice that even mild anxiety will rouse a nearly overpowering appetite.

***

The landscape of family is marked by love—but also by loss, by fear and by joy, and by the wash of more ordinary, gentler emotions amid those more dramatic peaks. Emotion sears memory, and memories map the way of family. It's been six years since I wrote that journal account, and two years since our daughter turned thirty. Our kids have moved into new jobs, new relationships, marriage, adventures of all kinds. The youngest has, across this time and against the odds, regained his balance, grown even stronger, becoming a young man full of promise.

Looking back across those years, it feels as if we gathered ourselves around him, hand to hand, extending whatever small comfort our caring, our love, could provide. Others braced him, in other ways, and they, in turn, have become special to us. It was—is still—a tricky business: to extend support, pulling back when what was support becomes constraining, straining the very bonds it was meant to foster.

But looking after each other, no matter how turbulent or how fraught with risk, also deepens love; allows or *makes* us speak of it when we otherwise would retreat, grow lazy, or hide in the weeds of simpler sentiments.

***

Like the rest of us, our younger son takes joy in cooking. He told me his girlfriend sometimes will bake him a lemon meringue pie. What a lovely irony: Lemon meringue is one pie I never made, but on road trips when the kids were small, this boy would always order it. Where did he even know it from? Not home. I'm not sure he can bring himself to eat a bite of pie, still; but he will cherish the fact that it was made for him and accept the sweet gift. He'll appreciate it, share it with friends, and love that she made it for him. For her, he makes roast chicken and pork tenderloins, casseroles and soups of all kinds. He's proud of his proficiency with bread and stock.

***

It surprised me how love will surge from the shallows, engulfing us when we least expect it. Love binds us, and yet for months at a time we'll barely notice—or speak of it. Driven by love, I say too much, or too little, and probably at the wrong times; out of love we do irrational and erratic things—things like making a pie, or baking cookies, or keeping secrets.

Sometimes those small acts of love will help, and other times, they will injure. Often, the things we do, swept along in love's current, will be utterly useless. But we persist. And every now and then some blundering little act of love may just lend relief. Love of family: as simple as a plate of homemade sweets, as unpredictable as a recipe, as friable as cookie crumbs.

GRAVITY'S PUSH

One morning last week I was walking across our campus, on a paved path, when suddenly I wasn't. Instead, I was face down, sprawled out on the path. Beyond the unpleasant surprise, there was an element of slapstick to the moment. I've been preoccupied with the idea of gravity lately. It's entirely possible that I missed a crack in the pavement and lost my balance all because gravity was on my mind. There's nothing else to explain why I fell.

I am prone to inattention—which does not combine well with another of my tendencies: moving too fast. That combination does result in the odd awkward collision. But as an adult, upright is my normal state of being.

As a kid, it was a different story. That recent fall—with the attendant bloodied knuckles, scraped palm, and bruised knee—takes me right back to childhood. As a kid, falling was commonplace. I have the scars to prove it: indented crosshatching below one knee (railroad trestle); outline of a tooth in lower lip (icy hill plus flying saucer); gash on right elbow (makeshift skateboard). I attribute those frequent mishaps to an excess of energy, combined with a deficiency of coordination and a healthy dose of myopia.

I don't remember those falls causing any sense of shock or betrayal; only momentary disappointment, and maybe a delay to our playing to scrounge up a Band-Aid. No big deal. And always best to evade parental attention (with its imminent risk to shut down the diversion-at-hand, and also to call down the wrath of an irritated parent).

Falling will become usual again, I suspect, with age. My mother would take a few falls in her middle nineties. She banged and bruised herself, frightening us, though the blessing is that she hardly seemed to remember falling. The causes, I'd learn, include slower reflexes, changes in vision, loss of muscle, reduced sensitivity of nerves.

The decades spanning childhood and old age, then, might be considered my years of navigating through space—of resisting gravity—with whatever poise and predictability we can summon. Yet one more grace I seldom have the wit to appreciate. This is what's been on my mind.

***

Does gravity push or pull? I've hardly keyed in the question before I am pulled right into the debate playing out, courtesy of University of Cambridge, in the forum of *The Naked Scientist*.

No one really knows what gravity is, let alone if it pushes us down, or draws us upward. Every supposition leads only to another question, despite the brightest minds engaging the mysteries of gravity. The debate transcends mortality, with bloggers invoking Newton, Einstein, and Tesla. An ageless debate.

Yet watch a child on a trampoline and the starkest implications leap into focus. Over and over they push off and are drawn back earthward. We know gravity for the sway of our bodies, for our inability to withstand its force beyond the arc that traces our wilful and boisterous acts of resistance.

***

And what of age? Does age push or pull? Suck us earthward, or propel us outward?

This question, too, eludes us, remaining in the realm of mystery, though we do seem to worry more about aging, dedicating more energy to resisting its inevitable force. Grappling with age is a lonelier endeavour, too. Summon the image of that child on the trampoline, and you *know* that you have moved, one small moment at a time, toward mortality.

***

In the week after Christmas several years ago, we rented an oversized van and stuffed it full of ski and hockey gear, snacks and beer, and six of us (2 parents, 3 kids + boyfriend of the oldest) set off for Apex, a small resort a few hours south of home, in the interior of BC. Courtesy of a one-time bonus, we had purchased a stack of ski passes and rented a swank slope-side condo, complete with all the comforts of home, plus a few (big screen, ice-maker).

It was a near-perfect adventure. Aside from the boyfriend's bout of food poisoning (one prawn too many?), and a near crisis when, despite that massive screen, the TV offerings didn't include any sports' networks, it was uninterrupted fun. A pub solved one problem, bringing us passable pub food plus access to both World Juniors and the Canucks game, and with an alcove providing viewing for the youngest, a minor then who would also have been most devastated to miss any game. For our own activity (the whole point, after all), the kids played on the outside rink across from our condo, and in every combination, we variously skied, boarded, and skated.

I've never been a skater, but that was not going to hold me back. The whole point was to indulge, and that rare chance to see who we were away from the constraints of the familiar. From the rink extended this dazzlingly long, looping figure-eight of a track. How could I resist? On the evening of our second day, I borrowed my daughter's skates and made my way around the loops with my husband, a masterful skater, as ballast. For short stretches I did quite fine, but rounding to the base—unbalanced by rough ice—I grabbed at his hand, managing to steady myself and also nearly detaching his thumb from its joint.

My expectations of myself as a skater were sufficiently low to escape harm. Skiing, however, was the challenge I had anticipated with some trepidation. Skiing was *my* sport growing up, and though it had been thirty years since I'd actually skied, there were memories of competence to live up to. It was some comfort that my expectations, and those memories, were private. We live near another small resort, where our kids have grown up skiing with their dad, but for whatever series of small decisions which take on the look of choice, I had left Alpine for Nordic. Our kids have never known me to ski. They found the very idea of it entertaining.

It didn't take long to discover that shorter skis are pretty cool for manoeuvrability, but that—despite three decades of technological advance—ski boots tethered by alpine bindings are as impossible to walk in as they ever were. In that respect, the family was at least equally disabled as we slogged together toward the lift. At the top of the trails I was pleased—and relieved—to recognize, within moments, that solidly intermediate ability I had cultivated in the seventies.

Those short skis I'd rented were also rounded, resembling two small snowboards. With their blunted tips and my casual control, I would soon learn that one can, indeed, even get turned around and take part of a slope backwards.

***

Five years have changed a lot, but memory only requires the nudge of words, reread from an old Christmas letter, to spin from vague to vivid.

I remember the pull of gravity drawing me down that slope, backwards. And it was a rush, once I'd resigned myself to this new development in skiing. It could have been remarkable, a fine stunt, had it only been intentional. That fleeting thought was followed by another: that my son might glance back and see me—and be impressed. The sensation of backing down Apex was surprising, yes, but also exhilarating... until some protuberance I didn't see (a shortcoming of backwards skiing), caught an edge and took me down.

Gravity, for that whole sweet day, had been my friendly foe. I had delighted in resisting its force on run after run, weaving my way down trails in the midst of family, carving turns by relying on arch and edge of ski, manipulated by flex and impulse the body coaxes from muscle, mind, and memory. Now, on our final run—body pleasantly spent, mind in resting mode—gravity pulled its punch. Until this particular moment, it had propelled me down the slope upright, if momentarily backwards. No longer the playfully opposing force, gravity now flung me downward face first, pinning me to that slope.

Pushing against the frozen hill, I tried with all my muscle and wit to push off from the ground, but without twisting a troublesome left knee, straining weak wrists, or aggravating an already aching shoulder. With neither knees, wrists, nor shoulders, I had all the manoeuvrability of a sack of grain. Even less aplomb. Would I dare let go this last bit of resistance and slither down to the base, prone?

Gravity was at least a patient adversary. I took time to consider my choices: sacrifice a joint or two; slide down like a big coward; or stay put until hypothermia gently claimed me. This 3rd option was growing in appeal when a young man swooshed in alongside me, asking if I'd like a hand. He looked about 20, the age of my older son, who was likely in the lift line, starting to wonder where his mother could be. The young man at my side, though agile and confidently planted on the slope, seemed less at ease socially, perhaps unsure if he might have embarrassed me, or intruded. I did consider releasing him with some made-up assurance that I was fine—just taking a break. But I relinquished the remainder of my pride and admitted that my knee was locked and I could use a pull upright. He responded by digging an edge in and extending an arm. I pulled myself up against his grip, hoping against hope that his shoulder and wrist would bear their share of my weight, so I would not take gravity's side and bring him down too. I'm sure I out-weighed him, certainly with all the dampness I'd absorbed while prone.

***

The vivid memory of that adventure of a Christmas past got a boost by its association to a more recent Christmastime adventure—yet another tussle with gravity.

It's December and I'm on my familiar skinny skis, gliding around our lake, minutes from home. This time, I'm alone, taking refuge from a house brimming with family. It's the same family, but three intervening years has taken the kids further from our trajectory, and coming together now *becomes* the novelty, the adventure. It's hard to admit, even to myself, that while the pull of family draws me in to them, it also propels me out to my own solitary ways. Like gravity, I suppose, it's sometimes difficult to determine what pushes and what pulls at us. For now, however, I've relinquished to my need to restore myself and get out alone. It's been sweet and I'm ready—eager—to go back, and happily making my way to where the car's parked in the half-light of late afternoon.

Along the far side of the lake the snow had been brittle and fast. But on the south side, still slushy from the afternoon sun, the skiing is trickier, inconsistent, and I'm growing tired. I slip on an icy patch and regain balance. Too late I realize there's dampness seeping into the tracks.

The skis ice up, but the body still pitches forward in expectation of speed that's not realized. The skis drag to a stop and I'm down, prone on the ice. My skis V out to either side, with my body prone between. I kick up my knees and swing the skis to one side.

From this position, for anyone even slightly more agile, it would take nothing to spring upright and be gone. Someone stronger might knock bindings from ski boots, making standing a simpler endeavour. For me, I may as well be nailed to the surface of this familiar lake. My knees might take the wrenching motion and with an assist from elbow and then shoulder, I would likely have the capacity to heave myself up just fine. But I know the wretched vulnerability of these joints. Recovery can outlast seasons, taking down whole capacities. It's no longer mere gravity I resist, but that other pull, of aging, and immeasurably harder still, aging with grace—for which, to me, working joints seem a minimal requirement.

In fact, the body came through and I am happy to report that I didn't die there, on the shore of Heffley Lake, of hypothermia and lost dignity (though the thought passed through my mind). I did manage to right myself, arching upward by virtue of a reliance on my obliques, those underutilized abdominal muscles whose name I knew from a fitness class instructor (who, small blessing I now realize it to be, has forced me to attend to them). Those muscles generated just enough momentum to propel me upward, freeing me from gravity's grip. My left side would feel the strain for days, but muscles have more resilience than joints. The joints, spared from the rescue, kick in for the more ordinary effort of skiing homeward, back to family, where I will rejoice in our being together and, in a private moment of satisfaction, for persisting in the face of those ageless mysteries that push and pull at us.

Acknowledgements

I'm grateful to the small presses and journals who sustain the craft and bring the writing to readers. Thank you, in particular, to the prior publishers of five of the book's essays (or slightly varied versions of those essays).

"Bands" appeared in the "Facts and Arguments" section of *The Globe and Mail* in April 20, 2014 (as "My wedding ring has the 34-year itch").

"Gravity's Push," was published on December 14, 2017, in *Cargo Literary Magazine.*

"Changing Places," was published in *DASH* (Issue 13) in May of 2020.

"Collecting Thoughts on Memory" was published by *CRAFT* (Winter 2021), edited by the wonderful Katelyn Keating and Jacqueline Doyle.

"In Place" is included in the *Being Home*, an essay anthology edited by Sam Pickering (a long-time hero of mine) and Bob Kunzinger, published in 2021 by Madville.

Pulling this book together in a year as extraordinary as the past twelve months have been would never have happened were it not for Atmosphere Press. I'm grateful for the energy and professionalism, and the wholehearted spirit of Kyle McCord, Beste Miray Doğan, Kelleen Cullison, Cameron Finch, Lennie DeCerce, Nick Courtright, and the entire team at Atmosphere.

I've long been enthralled by the craft of the personal essay, and am thankful to many for an ever-deepening appreciation of the genre. A special thank you to four fellow essay writers: Jane Silcott, Shaun Hunter, Susan Olding, and Theresa Kishkan. I've been moved and inspired by their writing, and been privileged to enjoy their company and to learn from them.

I also want to thank the generous and opinionated members of our little writing group, friends and colleagues with whom, over the years, I've been privileged to share the acts of writing and reading essays. They've contributed to the pleasure of both. A special thank you to Lyn Baldwin, Susie Safford, Nancy Flood, and Dian Henderson, who influenced the shaping and revising of the essays within this collection.

This year in particular, with its many challenges, reminds us all of the significance of home and family, friendship and community: aspects of our lives more easily overlooked in 'normal' times. More than ever, connections with family and with a small core of friends has sustained me. A special thanks to those close friends (you know who you are), who've kept connected, sharing stories of home and work, exchanging books and articles, ideas, hope, and fears—and yes, fun and laughs, too.

Family is the heart of the book, and it's such a joy to turn to mine now. More thanks than words can express to Monty, partner, co-parent and co-grandparent, first reader, primary driver, and the one without whom none of this would ever have come to be. And to James, Andrew, and Nicole, a huge and heartfelt thank you: for who you are, for the extraordinary journey we've taken together, and for letting me share our stories.

About Atmosphere Press

Atmosphere Press is an independent, full-service publisher for excellent books in all genres and for all audiences. Learn more about what we do at atmospherepress.com.

We encourage you to check out some of Atmosphere's latest releases, which are available at Amazon.com and via order from your local bookstore:

Convergence: The Interconnection of Extraordinary Experiences, a book by Barbara Mango and Lynn Miller
Sacred Fool, a biography by Nathan Dean Talamantez
My Place in the Spiral, a photographic memoir by Rebecca Beardsall
My Eight Dads, a memoir by Mark Kirby
Vespers' Lament, essays by Brian Howard Luce
Without Her: Memoir of a Family, by Patsy Creedy
One Warrior to Another, a memoir by Richard Cleaves
Emotional Liberation: Life Beyond Triggers and Trauma, nonfiction by GuruMeher Khalsa
The Space Between Seconds, a book by NY Haynes
License to Learn, a book by Anna Switzer, PhD
The Bond, a memoir by A. M. Grotticelli
Sex—Interrupted: Igniting Intimacy While Living With Illness or Disability, a book by Iris Zink and Jenny Palter
Between Each Step: A Married Couple's Thru Hike On New Zealand's Te Araroa, a memoir by Patrice LaVigne

About the Author

Photograph by Jen Randall

Elizabeth Templeman lives in the south-central interior of British Columbia, in the same home where she and her husband started their family. She continues to enjoy teaching at Thompson Rivers University. Pastimes and passions include running (ever-more slowly), swimming in lakes or skiing their frozen surfaces, and cooking, baking, and gardening. She has a life-long love affair with words. Her first book was *Notes from The Interior: Settling in at Heffley Lake*, an earlier collection of essays. Individual essays, articles, and book reviews have appeared in various journals, reviews, anthologies, and newspapers.

CPSIA information can be obtained
at www.ICGtesting.com
Printed in the USA
BVHW072003211021
619240BV00002B/150